Advance Praise for
The Twilight Rounds

"Boxing expert and Serling aficionado Christopher Benedict is quite literally the only person who could have written this book. Rod Serling loved the sweet science and admired fighters and now, thanks to Chris, we have the first book that dissects Serling's meditations on the sport far beyond just *Requiem for a Heavyweight*. This is a knockout piece of work."
—**Nicholas Parisi, President of The Rod Serling Memorial Foundation and author of *Rod Serling: His Life, Work, and Imagination***

"From his first published piece in a post-WWII college literary magazine, through a writing career that paralleled the Golden Age of Television, Rod Serling, best known for his work on the phenomenally successful *The Twilight Zone* series, also possessed a lifelong passion for boxing. As a writer, he identified with fighters, who both knew that 'win, lose, or draw—you left everything you had to give on the blood- splattered canvas or the typewritten paper.' Christopher Benedict's new book, *The Twilight Rounds: Rod Serling Explores the Dark Side of Boxing*, seamlessly intertwines a fascinating biography of Serling's short life, with a well-sourced, enjoyably cerebral, and engagingly visual examination of Serling's unforgettable boxing-related stories and characters of page and screen."
—**Catherine Johnson, boxing historian and author of *Then the World Moved On: The Brutal Truth Behind the Max Baer-Frankie Campbell Fight***

"Christopher Benedict's new book, *The Twilight Rounds: Rod Serling Explores the Dark Side of Boxing*, focuses on a writer who once proclaimed, 'I've always liked fighting and fighters.' The beauty of Benedict's book is that it is more than just a biography of Serling the writer. Of course, we learn about his life, but Benedict also goes on to look at Serling's influence on writers that came after him. We are also given profiles of a variety of fascinating characters in some way connected to the man himself or his work. Reading Benedict's book, with Christopher as our expert guide through the boxing-related stories and characters that Serling created, is a highly informative and entertaining journey. He has done a fine job in bringing his subject to life; both Serling's work and the man behind the typewriter."

—**Steve Hunt, host of** *The Boxing Movie Podcast* **and author of** *Heavyweight Title Fights of the 1980s,* **https://www.stevehuntboxing.com/blog**

"Few writers have portrayed the degradations that boxing enacts on the body and soul with the profound empathy of screenwriter Rod Serling. Bless Chistopher Benedict for reacquainting us with this in *The Twilight Rounds,* and for his impassioned toil in providing us with the story behind the story of his journey through the world of smelly cigars and cauliflowered ears."

—**Mark Kram, Jr., author of** *'Smokin' Joe: The Life of Joe Frazier*

"A fascinating look at how Rod Serling's time in the boxing world left a lasting mark on his writing; shaping the tension, resilience, and moral complexity found throughout *The Twilight Zone,* but also impacting future writers who would take a page from Serling's writing manual. Here, Christopher Benedict reveals how the grit of this sport fueled Serling's storytelling and how he used stories and characters from the ring to create vastly different tales. It certainly managed to draw me in to that world – even as someone with no boxing knowledge whatsoever!"

—**Emi O'Sullivan, co-Host of** *The After-Hours Podcast*

The Twilight Rounds

Rod Serling Explores the Dark Side of Boxing

Written by
Christopher Benedict

Foreword by
Anne Serling

Foreword by
Malissa Smith

Foreword by
Lady Tyger

Cover by
Koren Shadmi

Illustrations by
Tina Yoogin

JOBBER HOUSE
PRESS

The Twilight Rounds:
Rod Serling Explores the Dark Side of Boxing

Cover by Koren Shadmi
Illustrations by Tina Yoogin
Interior design and formatting by Amanda Bunch
Editorial consulting by Geremy Stone

ISBN (paperback) 979-8-9886092-4-7
ISBN (e-book)   979-8-9886092-5-4
ISBN (audiobook) 979-8-9886092-6-1

Library of Congress Control Number: 2025915717

Published by Jobber House Press, LLC
www.JobberHouse.com

Table of Contents

Acknowledgments

Had it not been for the support, encouragement, and guidance of Nicholas Parisi, this labor of love would probably be nothing more than a pile of papers defaced by my chicken scratch handwriting crammed into a bulging manila file folder. Nick is not only the President of the Rod Serling Memorial Foundation, but he literally wrote the book on the man. He is also a fellow Long Islander and one of the most humble and knowledgeable guys you could ever hope to meet. Thank you, Nick, for responding to my initial pitch for this idea at Book Revue with enthusiasm, supplying me with research material, and patiently answering my multitude of questions along the way. I couldn't have done this without you in my corner.

My profuse and sincere gratitude to Anne Serling for giving this project her blessing, which set me off on my journey with an extra spring in my step. Anne's memoir, *As I Knew Him: My Dad, Rod Serling*, is an intimate and beautiful remembrance of her father that you will find nowhere else. It is a must- read for any fan of *The Twilight Zone* creator who wants to get to know Rod Serling the father, the family man, the practical joker. Anne, it was an honor to have met you at the SerlingFest events in 2019 and 2024, and I thank you for all you do to keep your father's legacy alive and well.

Many thanks to *The Twilight Zone Haiku* author Chad Boykin for sharing a table with me in the memorabilia room at SerlingFest 2024, organizing a book signing event at the Vestal Barnes & Noble to kick off the weekend, and encouraging me to do this new edition of *The Twilight Rounds* with Jobber House Press. I always enjoy our lively conversations about Rod Serling and boxing.

A tip of the cap to Mike Goodpaster and Jeremiah Preisser, my former editors at *The Grueling Truth*, for originally going along with this idea, which ran as an eight-part series during the Covid lockdown of 2020 when there obviously wasn't any current boxing news to report on. Soon after, Nick Parisi first suggested that I compile the individual stories into book form. Following his lead, I self-published a handful of copies that I gave out as gifts and donated to the Rod Serling Memorial Foundation for the fundraiser during that summer's virtual SerlingFest.

This passion project has since taken on a life of its own thanks in part to the support of fellow Zoners and Serling fanatics Tony Albarella, Marc Barnhill, Jim Benson, Joanna Brumley, Mark Dawidziak, Tom Elliot, Lee Fernandes, Gail Flug, Paul Gallagher, Helen and Johnny Holmes, Tracey Loubier, Joel Lutenberg, Michael Lynn, Cassandra May, Terry Meichner, Igor Carastan Noboa, Mike Pipher, Andrew Polak, Kenneth Brian Sall, Rachel Schwab, Scott Skelton, Lisa Smith-Wilson, Andy Valentine, and Shelley McKay Young.

Special shoutouts as well to my brothers and sisters in boxing: Sumya Anani, Alicia Ashley, Iran Barkley, Jeff Brophy, Darlene Buckskin, Georgina Cammalleri, Jimmy Finn, Sue Fox, Thomas Gerbasi, Steve Hunt, Cat Johnson, Eva Jones- Young, Mark Jones, Sparkle Lee, Bonnie Mann, Joanne Metallo, Eddie Montalvo, Diego Morilla, Michael Nunn, Gerry O'Toole, Susan Reno, Yvonne 'Stringbean' Scott, John 'Iceman' Scully, Chris Smith, Malissa Smith, Carmen Sosa, Britt VanBuskirk, Cora Webber, and Ty Williams. My apologies to anyone I unintentionally left off either list.

I cannot fail to mention my fellow Bozos—Len Costello, Chris De-Chick, and Rick Gagne—who make the International Boxing Hall of Fame induction weekends in Canastota so much fun. They are a big reason why I keep returning year after year.

With the inspiration of Rod Serling, I have made it this far through life aided by a moral compass which is always set to true north. I have been a *Twilight Zone* enthusiast since I was a little boy. Rod Serling was not only my trusted tour guide through the fifth dimension, but a phenomenally talented writer, a man of unwavering principles who didn't merely talk the talk but walked the walk at a breakneck pace. I even considered him something of a father figure. Still do.

Rod Serling, this book is dedicated to you, although I'm sure you won't mind sharing the honor with my mom, Clare Szczygiel, who, like you, died at the tragically young age of 50. Mom, it was you who taught me how to be a fighter and get up off the floor with a renewed sense of purpose when life kicks the shit out of you. I couldn't possibly love or miss you more.

To my brother and partner in crime, Kevin, who was also taken from us entirely too soon—you will always be the coolest, smartest, most adventurous guy I ever knew.

This is also for Beea, Wren, Marc, Vlasta, Nalo, and Corrina for being the most amazing family I could have hoped for.

Last but certainly not least, this book is dedicated with love and utmost respect to my best friend and all-time favorite boxer, Lady Tyger. You too, Baby and BB.

And now, submitted for your approval… *The Twilight Rounds*. Enjoy the journey!

Foreword
by Anne Serling

Christopher Benedict has written a new book about boxing, *The Twilight Rounds*. This is his seventh book about the subject. He clearly knows what he's talking about.

As a bit of history, I first met Chris at a SerlingFest event, perhaps a decade ago. We met again in 2024. Suffice it to say, it is not his knowledge about boxing that made me agree to write him a foreword. It is a combination of Chris' genuine kindness (a growing rarity in today's world) and his clear respect for my father and his works.

I should confess right now that I know woefully little about boxing. When my father died at 50, I had just turned twenty. In those years, I was aware that shortly after my dad enlisted in the war (WWII) he boxed in a training camp to make a little money and earn privileges. I knew that his nose had been broken twice—he would point to it showing me the exact places he had been hit.

I remember too, when I was perhaps 10, my father play-boxing with me in the hall of our old house in California. I can still see us there, my dad's hands up in the air, quick moves and me clueless about what to do, despite his instructions. Let's just say, lacking the skill and the patience, I was not the protégé he may have hoped for. And certainly not the scene my dad may have been trying to reenact when Mountain in my father's script "Requiem for a Heavyweight" teaches a little boy how to throw a punch. I was a lousy study.

But one doesn't need to be an authority on boxing to be interested in *The Twilight Rounds*. What Chris masterfully does in this extraordinary book is weave my father's lifelong attraction to boxing together with interesting background information and stories.

Of my dad's early works, Chris says: "With the benefit of hindsight, it is very easy to see how the 23-year-old Serling used the story "The Good Right Hand" to sow the seeds he would nurture throughout the creative process of tending to his future boxing stories until they reached full maturity and blossomed eight years later into "Requiem for a Heavyweight.""

In his carefully appointed chapters, Chris not only demonstrates my dad's affection for boxing and for the human being behind the gloves but also for my father's deep love and concern for humanity as a whole.

In my father's commentary for his script "Requiem for a Heavyweight," my dad wrote that he had one basic premise while writing "Requiem" and that was: "Every man can and must search for his own personal dignity."

Thank you, Chris. With your own dignity, you have brought my dad's works and words back to life with meticulous care. I am so appreciative.

Anne Serling is the daughter of Rod Serling and serves on the Board of Directors for the Rod Serling Memorial Foundation. She is author of the memoir *As I Knew Him: My Dad, Rod Serling* and contributed adaptations of two of her father's scripts to *The Twilight Zone: The Original Stories* anthology. Anne is the founder and an Editorial Board member of Rod Serling Books, an independent publishing house whose mission is to make his otherwise out of print works available and affordable. "The Big, Tall Wish" (*More Stories from the Twilight Zone*) and both the original teleplay (collected in *Patterns*) and movie tie-in novelization for *Requiem for a Heavyweight* are among them.

Foreword
by Malissa Smith

I admit to having a complicated relationship with Rod Serling's work. Watching *The Twilight Zone* episodes as a kid was unnerving at best. They were filled with irony, pain, sorrow, and a worldview tempered by war, red scares, racism, and the ever-present threat of nuclear annihilation that was a Cold War upbringing in the 1950s and 1960s.

In Christopher Benedict's brilliant ten-round biography of Rod Serling's life, we are treated to the extraordinary pathos of boxing as the lens to view a champion's life of hard work, improvisational brilliance with the tools of his writing trade, and the ability to take a beating into unconsciousness, something anyone who has ever been in the ring knows only too well. Each chapter is a round in Serling's life interwoven with the important pivot points and how they informed his writing interspersed with the lives of boxers who influenced Serling's stories.

Benedict also makes linkages between Serling's searing ring experiences and the warrior's code he brushed against becoming a Purple Heart recipient fighting the Japanese in World War Two. We are shown the 21-year-old returning veteran, battered by war, plagued by nightmares, and ready to embrace his life's work as a writer in order, as Benedict tells us, to expel the bitterness he felt at his experiences. Beginning with Serling's short story, "The Good Right Hand," published in his college's literary magazine, *The Antiochian*, Benedict critiques Serling's boxing stories as metaphors for the complex emotional landscape of disappointment that can lead even to suicide. But it is in writing about Serling's prolific, unrelenting work ethic, that one comes to understand his intensity, as if he were fighting end-to-end in each of the three-minute round increments of a boxing match.

Benedict interweaves the biographical pivot points of Serling's life with beautifully rendered snapshots of boxers such as Tony Canzoneri, whose fight career spanned from 1925-1939 with a record of 137-24-10. Benedict tells us he was a crowd-pleasing fighter typical of Serling's boxing characters: A real-life fighter who won titles, lost titles, was the recipient of bum decisions, and in his final outing was down once before being counted out. Becoming an actor, Canzoneri, appeared in two of Serling's boxing inspired scripts, "The Face of Autumn" for *Lux Video Theater*, on CBS in 1952, and

CHRISTOPHER BENEDICT

"The Twilight Rounds", a pivotal boxing drama which appeared on NBC's *Kraft Theater* in 1953. This brought a verisimilitude to the story lines which were unparalleled in rendering the truths of the boxing world.

As one of the "angry young men" of television in such company as Paddy Chayefsky and Horton Foote, Serling's Emmy win for his 1955 teleplay "Patterns" broke new ground for what Benedict calls an "impassioned, scathing indictment," of the soul crushing ruthlessness of the business world. While a non-boxing story, it had obvious parallels to the exploitation of fighters he would return to repeatedly throughout his career, including his script for his next great triumph, "Requiem for a Heavyweight," starring Jack Palance as Harlan 'Mountain' McClintock in the CBS *Playhouse 90* live television show in October 1956.

In summing up this brilliant work, Benedict chooses to quote Serling himself who said it was "as honest a piece as I've ever done." Benedict also treats us to his perspective of the script intermingled with the real-life stories of boxers and hangers on whose lives informed the layered nuances of the teleplay. We are also shown the impact of the script on television as a medium, and in a subsequent Round, the story behind further performances of the script world-wide and the 1962 film treatment starring Anthony Quinn as Mountain.

Benedict's Round Seven gives us what we've been waiting for, our first glimpse of Serling's iconic series, *The Twilight Zone*. True to the book's lens of boxing, however, the chapter's focus is on the 27th episode of the series' first season, televised in April 1960 and entitled "The Big Tall Wish." While a boxing story, Benedict also informs us that in choosing to render the script from the viewpoint of an African American boxer with mostly Black characters, Serling stressed the story as a "counterpoint to the harmful stereotypes so prevalent then."

The chapter goes on to discuss two other scripts, "The Four of Us are Dying" and "Steel" along with Benedict's signature rendering of the backstories behind the scripts along with his critiques and summaries of the storylines. Throughout the rounds of the book, Benedict not only delves into Serling's life but also gives us the interrelationships with the actors who portrayed characters, the production processes, the work with other writers, producers, and directors, the impact on Serling's further development and career, and his own critiques of his work.

Where Benedict's work shines, however, is in rendering the boxing life in parallel with Serling's writings. Benedict always returns to the lives of boxers whether as performers or influences on the final product, not to mention Serling's own unique perspective as a former boxer. Against the backdrop of the microcosm of the business of boxing, Benedict shows us Serling's indictment of a harsh and unforgiving world and in quoting Serling in his speech to the Library of Congress in 1968 gives truth to Serling's perspective that "the writer's role is to menace the public's conscience."

Benedict sums it up in Round Ten, writing and boxing are ultimately solitary pursuits, Serling likely drew many parallels between the mindset of one and the other which correspond in a unique and quite meaningful way.

Would that any of us should have lived such an honorable and just life.

Malissa Smith is an accomplished historian and author. She is a member of the Ring magazine women's ratings panel, an elector with the International Boxing Hall of Fame, and serves on the board of directors for the International Women's Boxing Hall of Fame, hosting their annual induction ceremony. Malissa is the author of *A History of Women's Boxing* and its follow-up, *The Promise of Women's Boxing*, both considered essential in the field, and contributed the essay, "How Boxing Uncaged Me" for the book *The Difference: Essays on Loss, Courage, and Personal Transformation*. Her blog, Girlboxing.org, has been online since 2010.

CHRISTOPHER BENEDICT
Foreword
by Lady Tyger

Well, hello there. Let me introduce myself.

I'm Marian Trimiar, better known as Lady Tyger. I won the Women's World Lightweight Championship in 1979 and was one of the first females to receive a boxing license in the state of New York. I went on a hunger strike to bring attention to the plight of women boxers and was inducted into the International Boxing Hall of Fame in 2022.

I could go on and on about my struggles and accomplishments, but this is not about me. This is about my best friend and author extraordinaire who wrote the book *The Twilight Rounds*.

I met Chris through a friend of mine named Sue Fox. Sue and I call each other "sis" because we both lost our sisters. She runs WBAN and is one of the biggest advocates for women's boxing. Sue Fox called me and told me about Christopher Benedict, the man who wrote a story about me. I saw the story and was extremely impressed with his writing. We finally communicated by text and phone. We've been friends for over five years. We are super close friends and super platonic. He's a super cool dude and is loved.

Chris is a writer, journalist, and activist. He's studied and written about slavery, civil rights, and knows more about Black history than most. He's also an advocate for women's boxing. He's written many books about women's boxing, researching its history and documenting our struggles and achievements. He's knowledgeable on boxing and an avid fan of Mr. Serling and *The Twilight Zone*.

Here's something Chris and Rod have in common: they are both writers, journalists, and activists. Most people don't know that Mr. Serling organized boycotts and made sure Blacks were on his show *The Twilight Zone*. And he's in good company with other white people who supported Black people.

Namely: Eleanor Roosevelt, who invited Marian Anderson to sing at the White House and arranged for her to give a concert at the Lincoln Memorial. I was named after Marian Anderson and was told I am related to her.

Ed Sullivan was a sportswriter, journalist, and activist. Mr. Sullivan provided a platform for African American entertainers on his popular TV show.

Mark Twain, like Rod Serling, was a journalist, writer, and activist, and so was Walter White. Rod Serling is in great company.

If people only knew about Rod, he's much more than *The Twilight Zone* and *Night Gallery*. Rod Serling was a boxing fan and actually boxed in the Army. Mr. Serling wrote "The Big, Tall Wish" for *The Twilight Zone* which featured several Black cast members. He also wrote "Requiem for a Heavyweight" which won a Peabody award and an Emmy. What a brilliant mind to think of *Night Gallery* and *The Twilight Zone*.

There was a big event in Binghamton, New York in 2024 celebrating Rod Serling's 100th birthday. They unveiled his statue during SerlingFest and Chris was one of the guest speakers at the event.

I'm a big fan of Chris, Rod, and *The Twilight Zone*. I was more than elated to write this foreword. If you're reading this foreword, please move forward to the cashier and purchase *The Twilight Rounds*. It will be a journey you'll enjoy.

Peace and Love, Lady Tyger.

Lady Tyger Trimiar is a former boxer who broke down gender and racial barriers in the sport in the 1970s and 80s. After four years of legal battles, Tyger was one of the first three women who were simultaneously granted professional boxing licenses by the New York State Athletic Commission in 1978. She competed in the first ever women's boxing matches held in Connecticut and Pennsylvania and headlined the inaugural all-female fight card in 1979, the same year she won the Women's World Lightweight Championship. A tireless advocate for women's rights, Trimiar went on a 30-day hunger strike in 1987 to publicize the boxing establishment's discriminatory practices. Lady Tyger's trailblazing career earned her inductions into both the International Women's Boxing Hall of Fame (Class of 2016) and International Boxing Hall of Fame (Class of 2021).

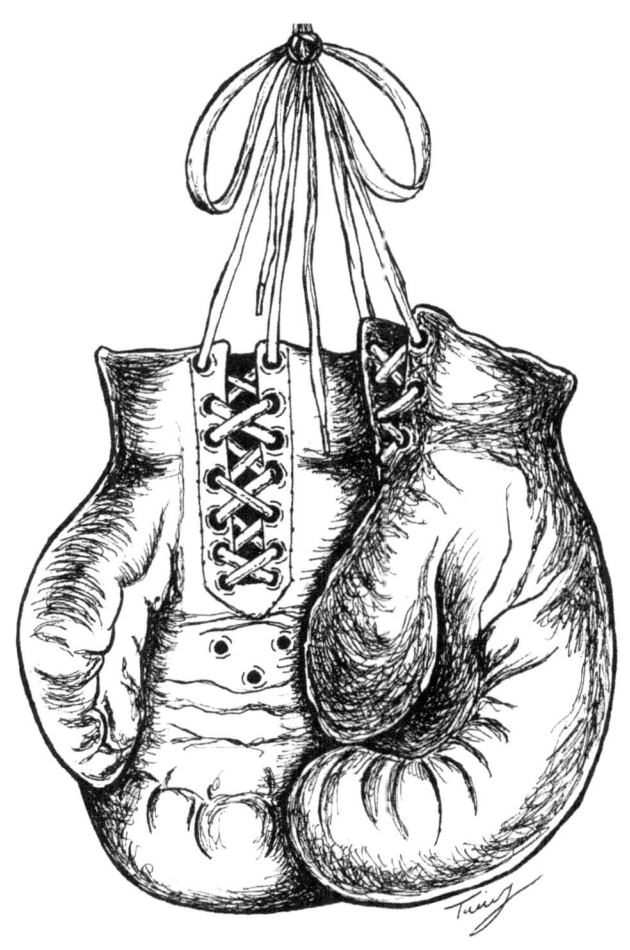

"...as long as they speak your name, you continue."
—**Rod Serling**

"Being like everybody is the same as being nobody"
—**Rod Serling**

Binghamton: Hometown to the Twilight Zone Creator, Birthplace of a Heavyweight Champion

Because he felt that a prizefighter was essentially treated like a "freak" by the profession and regarded as little more than a "battered hulk" by society, Rod Serling invoked the word "tragedy" time and again when explaining how the sport of boxing provides such fertile ground for dramatic interpretation.

Serling's love for boxing locked horns with his moral, at times cynical, worldview. He would spend two decades tilling the artistic soil of the fight racket, repeatedly turning it this way and that in an effort to unearth its more unseemly elements. Examining boxing as a cold, calculating, and uncaring enterprise, with the pugilist as its human stock in trade, became what Rod referred to as a "strange, haunting fascination."

Enthusiasts refer to boxing as "the sweet science," likening it to a brutal ballet or smashmouth chess game. The term itself is sometimes attributed to journalist A.J. Liebling, whose 1956 book by the same name is required reading for serious students of the fight game. Liebling, however, borrowed the phrase from 19th century British wordsmith Pierce Egan, who compiled five volumes of writings entitled *Boxiana* wherein he chronicled the exploits of the hardscrabble, bare-knuckled participants of what he called "the sweet science of bruising." Contained within those quotation marks lies boxing's paradox.

Antagonists argue that prizefighting is merely a blood sport with no redeeming value, insensibly barbaric and overripe for abolition. To the untrained eye, this seems like a perfectly rational way of viewing a vocation that requires its practitioners to bludgeon each other into a concussive state of incoherence and immobility which is intended—and hoped—to be temporary. But it is a disquieting truth that this specific brand of blunt force trauma carries a heavy cost.

Call them what you will: dreams of championship glory or delusions of grandeur. Either way a boxer's aspirations rack up debts which are often collected incrementally, an unfair payment plan spread out over the course of decades in the form of irreversible physical and mental decline. Sadly, in certain circumstances, the penalty can be called to account immediately. And fatally.

Yet, given close enough scrutiny and careful consideration, it becomes possible to develop an appreciation for the undeniable technical artistry inherent to the performances of the men and women who fearlessly lace up the gloves. Studying the poetic physicality of Sugar Ray Robinson, Muhammad Ali, Michael Nunn, Pernell Whitaker, Katie Taylor, and Vasiliy Lo-

3

machenko as they strive towards the fighter's creed to "hit and not get hit" is not unlike bearing witness to the graceful virtuosity of Mikhail Baryshnikov executing a series of flawless pirouettes or Carmen Amaya dancing the flamenco. Each requires what may appear to be reckless abandon but is instead a masterful demonstration of diligently practiced choreography complemented by a kinetic fluidity which is as inspired as it is spontaneous.

Boxers and chess players strategize in a similar fashion, formulating tactical game plans they hope to adhere to as they enter into combat while carrying with them the awareness that they will often be forced to improvise critical adapt-or-perish maneuvers when disadvantageous situations suddenly materialize. The preferred methodology depends upon the individual prizefighter or grandmaster. It might be to attack aggressively from the outset, thus dictating the pace and imposing your will on your opponent. Alternatively, it could begin deliberately with a small measure of caution that allows for the time and space necessary to assess the situation, weigh options, and, when the time is right, set a trap with malice aforethought intended to render a foe helpless to counter in another few moves or less. In this way, the likes of Joe Louis, Marvelous Marvin Hagler, and Mike Tyson are not far removed from Bobby Fischer, Garry Kasparov, and Magnus Carlsen.

True, Fischer was not called upon to deliver a blow to Boris Spassky's ribcage with the chess board during one of their classic tête-à-têtes, and Baryshnikov never had to concern himself with avoiding a left hook whistling past his temple while leaping across the stage.

Rod Serling, an athletic and aggressively competitive young man, was an active boxer during his military training. As a clinical and conscientious observer, however, he took a decidedly dim view of the so-called "sweet science" because of the cruel treatment dealt out to its participants beyond the confines of the ring, a merciless cause and effect of the savage punishment fighters inflict upon one another between the ropes.

Steeped in the tradition established by prestigious scribes such as George Bernard Shaw, Jack London, Ernest Hemingway, and Budd Schulberg before him, Serling would revisit the setting of the prize ring multiple times throughout his writing career—from its origins at Antioch College in print and on the radio, to the burgeoning medium of live television, to feature films, to the supernatural realms of *The Twilight Zone* and *Night Gallery*.

***

Anyone familiar with the autobiographical *Twilight Zone* episode "Walk-

 4

ing Distance," as well as its companion piece "A Stop at Willoughby," has a working knowledge of Serling's adult longing to do what Thomas Wolfe warned was impossible (or at best unwise) and go home again. Even if it was an itch he knew he could not scratch, he yearned to travel back to a peaceful, restful place where a man could live his life full measure, to revisit the childhood thrills of riding a merry-go-round and eating cotton candy while watching a band concert. For Serling, Binghamton was this place.

Rodman Edward Serling was born in Syracuse, New York on Christmas Day 1924. Before he had turned two, the family moved to Binghamton where his father Sam went into business as a grocer and, later, with the assistance of a young Rod making deliveries by bicycle, a butcher. The Serling's settled into a charming two-story house on Bennett Avenue, a stone's throw from Recreation Park where Rod would often ride the carousel or hang around the bandstand, both of which feature prominently in "Walking Distance."

Strolling through a close approximation of Recreation Park on the MGM backlot, Gig Young, as Martin Sloan, memorably and paradoxically encounters his younger self carving his initials into one of the gazebo's pillars. Serling isn't known to have done this as a boy, but he did paint his name on the wooden door frame over the entrance to the prop room backstage at Binghamton Central High School's performing arts theatre. It still survives today, recovered and kept safe for posterity.

Serling's boyhood home at 67 Bennett Avenue is about a mile and a half and a few twists and turns across town from Gerard Avenue, known as Maiden Avenue when one-time heavyweight champion Jack Sharkey grew up there. Born on October 26, 1902, to Lithuanian immigrants in Binghamton's First Ward, the future boxer was christened Joseph Paul Zukauskas.

Times were tough for the Zukauskas family at the turn of the century. Food was hard to come by and young Joseph took it upon himself to help heat their home with coal pilfered from the hoppers at the nearby railyard. Preferring to spend his time fishing rather than learning, he dropped out of school at the age of twelve and ran away from home as a teenager, crossing the Brooklyn Bridge with a nickel in his pocket and joining the Navy.

The ship he was assigned to was docked in Boston which Zukauskas would adopt as his hometown to become a New Englander from that point forward. It was a reversal of the way the Syracuse-born Rod Serling had attached himself to Binghamton throughout his formative years and forever after.

Zukauskas began boxing in the Navy, winning all but one of thirty-nine fights by his count and earning the title of Atlantic Fleet Champion. While preparing to turn pro, he was urged by a Boston fight club manager to alter his identity and opted for the moniker Jack Sharkey, a contraction of the names of his two pugilistic heroes. One was the heavyweight champion, Jack Dempsey. The other was Irish phenom Tom Sharkey, who, like his future namesake, had run away from home to join the Navy and subsequently taken part in thrilling knuckle-dusters with the best in the business—guys like Joe Choynski, James J. Jeffries, James J. Corbett, and Bob Fitzsimmons—winning some and losing some.

Sharkey, Jack that is, squared off against his idol Jack Dempsey on July 21, 1927, before 82,000 fight fans packed inside Yankee Stadium. The winner would hold the right to become the mandatory challenger to Gene Tunney, who had claimed the heavyweight title from Dempsey ten months prior. The rough and tumble Dempsey, who loved to break his antagonist down by slugging away at their midsection, hit Sharkey with a body blow in the seventh round which strayed well below the belt. Ignoring the exhaustively repeated directive to "protect yourself at all times," Sharkey turned away from his opponent to lodge a complaint with referee Jack O'Sullivan but found himself on the business end of a Dempsey left hook he never saw coming.

Though his immediate aspirations toward the world heavyweight title ended with the ten-count administered by the referee that night, Sharkey would again compete for the championship three years later against the dangerous German contender Max Schmeling in a bout which would also be determined by a foul. Gene Tunney, who defeated Dempsey in their rematch infamous for Tunney receiving a "long count" after Dempsey sent him to the deck in the seventh round, retired to leave the heavyweight championship vacant. It would be awarded to the winner of the bout between the division's top two contenders, Sharkey and Schmeling, at Yankee Stadium on June 2, 1930.

Sharkey, who had won the first three rounds, landed a shot south of Schmeling's waistline in the fourth which deposited the German challenger onto the canvas and propelled him to the world championship by way of disqualification. Schmeling's manager, Joe Jacobs, leapt onto the ring apron repeatedly yelling "foul!" and prompting Schmeling to writhe around in agony until the referee, former boxer Ed 'Gunboat' Smith, was left with little other choice. Neither man wished the fight to end this way, especially Schmeling, his victory tarnished by being dubbed the "low blow champion." And yet, Joe Jacobs refused Sharkey an immediate rematch which forced the hand of the New York State Athletic Commission in stripping Schmeling of their portion of the world title.

Schmeling would instead successfully defend his now-fractured crown against Young Stribling by way of technical knockout in the last of 15 scheduled rounds before granting Sharkey a return bout two years after their first dustup, on June 21, 1932, at the Madison Square Garden Bowl. Despite the popular consensus of ringside observers that Schmeling had done more than enough to outpoint his challenger, the two judges gave conflicting verdicts in favor of each fighter. The outcome was left in the hands of referee Gunboat Smith, who scored it for Sharkey and caused the title to change hands. Schmeling's Barnumesque manager Joe Jacobs, always one to seize the opportunity for an ostentatious display of showmanship, famously screamed "We wuz robbed!" into the microphone, introducing that phrase into boxing lexicon. It has been intimated that the fight was fixed, some sources allege even by Sharkey himself, though he denied it.

There was no doubt about the outcome of his first title defense. Or was there? 'The Ambling Alp,' six-foot-six Primo Carnera, whom Sharkey had previously outpointed in decisive fashion, knocked the new champion out with a right uppercut in the sixth round, ending Sharkey's brief reign as king of the heavyweights at one year and eight days. Did Sharkey take a dive for a short-term payoff? Like the dubious outcome of the second Schmeling bout, there have also been suspicions about this one.

Nevertheless, three years later rising superstar and soon-to- be heavyweight champion Joe Louis sent Sharkey into retirement courtesy of a third-round knockout. He would open his own watering hole in Boston, referee boxing and wrestling matches, and become fishing buddies with Red Sox legend Ted Williams. Jack Sharkey lived to be 91 years old.

Just as Sharkey had learned the "manly art of self-defense" during his stint in the military, Rod Serling took up boxing while attending jump school in Fort Benning, Georgia, where he trained to become a World War II paratrooper and demolition specialist. Despite his wishes to go to Europe and fight the Nazis, Rod was eventually deployed to the Japanese-occupied Philippines with the 511th Infantry, First Battalion, of the 11th Airborne Division.

As a teenager, Serling earned the reputation for being a terror with the ping pong paddle and tennis racket. Though having stood a mere five-foot-four, he had also brazenly tried out for the Binghamton Central High

School varsity football squad only to learn, as Rod later joked, that Coach Henry Merz preferred to have a quarterback who weighed more than the bulldog that served as the team mascot.

Private First Class Serling is said to have had more on his mind than monitoring world events in his spare time. His boyhood pal Norman Miller claimed that Rod wrote him letters bragging about getting locked up for picking fights with other servicemen at pubs in Columbus, Georgia. Perhaps in an effort to curtail his trainees' extracurricular donnybrooks, division commander General Raymond Swing organized sanctioned boxing tournaments which Serling would compete in with "seemingly masochistic glee."

Fighting in the flyweight class (108 to 112 pounds in the professional ranks, but this requirement possibly had some wiggle room in the military), Serling won his first seventeen bouts, scrapping his way to the second round of the divisional finals. His victories also won him a letter from his mother, Esther, congratulating him on being such a "tough lug," in her words, but begging him not to get his "good looking face all slammed up."

Unfortunately, in his eighteenth and final fight, that is precisely what happened. While attending maneuvers at Camp Polk in Louisiana, Serling was ponderously matched against a six-foot-two, 200-pound heavyweight by the name of Kelly who proceeded to pummel his hapless opponent into oblivion.

Serling wasn't able to so much as lay a glove on him, according to regiment mate Ken Haan. Vernon Hartung, a high school chum of Rod's who had been inducted into the Army alongside Serling at Fort Niagara, tended to his beaten and bloodied comrade before he lost consciousness.

Serling's daughter Anne recalls in her beautifully written memoir the time when her father pointed out to her where his nose was broken in two places as a result.

In response to a newspaper reporter who commended him for having "the ring in his blood," Serling stated pragmatically that he had spilled plenty of his own blood in the ring. So too did the characters who populated the boxing stories Rod Serling would write in due time.

ROUND 2

Antioch College: The Good Right Hand and To Live a Dream

When the question was put to him during what would turn out to be his last interview, conducted in March 1975 by Linda Brevelle, Rod Serling contemplated what it was exactly that compelled him to be a writer. Although he didn't feel in any way "anointed" by some higher power, Serling admitted to surrendering to a "sense of illusion," which would allow him to imagine being a "neutral beast" unable to fight off a sort of preordained impulse to write. He finished his thought by asserting that writers followed that distinct calling because of a need to say something that is "truthful and honest and pointed and important."

That Serling subscribed to this notion is something for which we can all be thankful. Charting the trajectory of when he did and why he did is critical in our comprehensive understanding of Rod Serling, both the creative force and the human being. The two were by no means mutually exclusive.

***

Technician Fourth Grade Rodman Edward Serling received an honorable discharge from the United States Army on January 13, 1946. He brought home with him the honors of the World War II Victory Medal, American Service Medal, Asiatic Pacific Service Medal with Arrowhead, Good Conduct Medal, Philippines Liberation Medal with Bronze Star, Parachutist Badge, Presidential Unit Citation, Republic of Philippines Unit Citation, and Purple Heart. But these ribbons and medals were far from the only reminders of his service.

Serling also came back to Binghamton with a negligibly disjointed nose courtesy of his misadventures inside the boxing ring as well as serious shrapnel wounds to his knee and wrist which earned him the Purple Heart. He would continue to walk with a slight limp and experience discomfort if not severe pain while typing for prolonged periods throughout the rest of his life.

Moreover, he had witnessed death and its consequences. Melvin Levy, his friend, was crushed by a freefalling crate during a drop on the Philippine Island of Leyte. He was also assigned to General Douglas MacArthur's Occupation of Japan outfit following the cessation of hostilities when his first sergeant committed suicide inside the agricultural school which served as their base of operations.

Serling once encountered an unnervingly close brush with mortality when he found himself in the crosshairs of a rifle brandished by a Japanese soldier taking dead aim at him. He would undoubtedly have been shot and killed if not for Richard, his quick-acting buddy who took out the enemy combatant from over Rod's shoulder.

By far, the most painful gut punch, existentially speaking, Serling received was the death of his beloved father Sam in September 1945, after the Japanese surrender but before his discharge. Because he had not accumulated the required number of points, Serling's request for personal leave to attend the services and be with his family back home at this terrible time was denied.

Many of Serling's post-war nights would be plagued by bad dreams. During occasional waking hours, he suffered the psychological effects of what is now diagnosed as post-traumatic stress disorder. Back then, it was simply and inadequately known as "shell shock." His daughter Anne remembers being woken up in the middle of the night to the sound of him screaming.

All things considered, Serling said that he arrived back home in Binghamton with a bitterness toward just about everything and that writing was the only way he knew how to expel it. The G.I. Bill provided Serling the opportunity to widen the scope of his academic horizon, which he initially intended to utilize in pursuit of a career in Physical Education. He was accepted into Antioch College, the progressive liberal arts school located in Yellow Springs, Ohio, that his older brother Robert had attended.

The institution's first president was the famous education reformer Horace Mann, whose motto "Be ashamed to die until you have won some victory for humanity" became a mission statement not only for the college but for Serling himself. The proof of how profoundly this message resonated with him is evidenced in the poignant *Twilight Zone* episode "The Changing of the Guard." The grounds of Serling's fictional Vermont preparatory Rock Spring School for Boys feature a Horace Mann statue adorned with that very quotation.

Carol Kramer was a pretty freshman with a double major in Elementary Education and Child Psychology when Serling first laid eyes on her on the Antioch campus. Her memory of having first seen Rod was of him impersonating a monkey, a favorite routine of his which would endlessly amuse his daughters Anne and Jodi around the Serling household in later years. Rod asked Carol out for coffee, and although she "thinks he is a bit of an idiot" as Anne tells it, his sense of humor and intelligence eventually won her over. They quickly became inseparable and were married on July 31, 1948.

Carol remained the diligent and loving gatekeeper to her husband's legacy to the very end when she passed away on January 9, 2020, at the age of 91. She also appears to have been a distant relation to Horace Mann, first cousins three times removed. Her grandfather was an Antioch trustee, and two of her great-grandfathers had been professors—of Chemistry and Natural History, respectively. Serling himself would return to his alma mater between November 1962 and January 1963, with the premiere of The Twilight Zone's fourth season looming right around the corner, to teach a course called Drama in the Mass Media.

⁎⁎➤

Haunted by wartime memories and troubled by social injustices, Serling felt an undeniable pull to give voice to his internal and external frustration and switched his major to Language and Literature. Under the tutelage of Paul Bentel, a radio scriptwriter, and Nolan Miller, Antioch's writer in residence, Serling began composing short stories and radio plays at a furious pace. He knew no other way.

When speaking with interviewer Linda Brevelle at one of his favorite restaurants, Franco's La Taverna on LA's Sunset Strip, Serling expressed that he would be honored to be remembered in a hundred years' time simply as "a writer." Not even as a famous, quotable writer. Just "a writer." That would suffice for him.

Sadly, just four months later Serling would die after undergoing open heart surgery at Strong Memorial Hospital in Rochester, New York. His humble wish to be remembered has unquestionably been granted honorably and exceeded by incalculable measure.

First mentored by his junior-high English teacher Helen Foley, Serling had served as writer and editor for *The Panorama*, which was the name of both Binghamton Central High School's student paper and yearbook. He also composed poetry while in the Army that he sent home for his sibling Robert to critique. Brutally honest in his assessment, Robert had to admit to his kid brother that he wasn't much of a poet. During his service, Serling had also come up with a radio skit to coincide with a visit from the USO featuring Bob Hope.

At Antioch, one of his earliest serious efforts was a lengthy war story entitled "First Squad, First Platoon," written with Serling's trademark intensity and augmented by the intimacy of a young man finding his way. There was also an immediacy to the piece undoubtedly stirred up by recent traumas. It certainly helped exorcise some personal demons, but the piece would not reach the public until appearing in *The Strand* magazine's Spring

2024 issue.

Instead, Serling's four-page boxing story that ran in the March 1948 edition of the school's literary magazine *The Antiochian* would become his first ever published piece of writing. We know now, of course, that much more would follow. The almost unimaginably prolific Serling would go on to establish a body of work that is extraordinary in every sense of the word and has fired the imagination of admirers and aspiring writers for decades. And it all started with "The Good Right Hand."

***

Swede emerges from the shower after winning the big title fight to find that his dressing room has become the site of an impromptu victory party. Fast-talking reporters, flashbulb-popping photographers, and fair-weather supporters are crammed together shoulder-to-shoulder and jostling for space closer to the new champ. This is all to the chagrin of Swede's manager, Googy Epstein, who seeks refuge from the pomp and circumstance in the adjacent locker room and encounters trainer Pop Trask.

When Pop compliments Swede's "powerhouse" of a right hand, Googy sinks into a somber, meditative mood as he thinks back to another boxer he had guided along previously. This fighter was Danny Fales, who had been a promising contender until he demolished his right hand on a ring post when Sailor Gibbons, trapped in the corner during their bout, slipped Danny's incoming punch. After that, Danny did little else besides sit around his room in a dingy boarding house examining his misshapen knuckles and mangled fingers while dwelling on what could have been but never was and never will be.

Googy pays his brooding ex-fighter a visit, telling Danny to stop feeling sorry for himself and consider a job as a warehouse inventory checker, a position that Googy had secured for him. Even better, they could scout out the local talent at Stillman's Gym and find an aspiring young boxer to work with together. Meaning well, Googy tells Danny that he needs him to be his right hand.

He becomes aware of the verbal blunder the moment the words were harmlessly expelled. Danny assures him that he understood Googy's kind intentions but still believes that life isn't worth living if he can't fight.

Fed up with Danny's emotional self-flagellation, Googy lays into him with some tough love. He not-so-subtly draws a parallel between Danny's current condition and his bout against Rodzynski in Cleveland when, despite both eyes being sealed shut, he continued throwing punches due to his instinct toward self-preservation. Danny reluctantly agrees to meet with Googy the next morning to discuss matters further.

Googy is having breakfast in a hotel coffee shop waiting for Danny and, almost as if guided by natural reflex, turns to the sports pages in the morning paper. He drops his coffee cup and rises from his seat in shocked disbelief upon seeing the headline reporting Danny Fales' death by suicide.

With the benefit of hindsight, it is very easy to see how the 23-year-old Serling used "The Good Right Hand" to sow the seeds he would nurture while tending to his future boxing stories. They would reach full maturity and blossom eight years later into "Requiem for a Heavyweight."

***

Serling wrote, directed, and acted in radio shows for the Antioch Broadcasting System, for which he would create an original anthology program and become station manager. As he was putting the finishing touches on his series in the spring of 1949, Serling was notified that one of his scripts, a boxing story called "To Live a Dream," had been chosen as one of several second-place winners in a nationwide contest. *Dr. Christian*, a CBS radio program with a reputation as "the only show on radio where the audience writes the scripts" and the sponsor of the contest, awarded Rod a cash prize of $500 and an all-expenses-paid trip to New York City for him and Carol.

During the presentation for the award, Serling would rub shoulders with third-time *Dr. Christian* contest winner Earl Hamner, Jr., who was there to be recognized for his story "All Things Come Home." This would be a serendipitous meeting as the two would collaborate on eight *Twilight Zone* episodes, including "The Hunt," "A Piano in the House," "Jess-Belle," and the series finale, "The Bewitchin' Pool," before Hamner, Jr. went on to create *The Waltons*.

Serling's *Dr. Christian* submission tells the tale of a former boxer who is losing his battle with leukemia. With the precious little time he has left, he strives to leave behind a legacy by imparting as much of his accumulated wisdom as he can onto the young fighter he is currently training.

Unfortunately, this short synopsis is currently all I can offer on the subject of "To Live a Dream." It is unknown whether Serling's script exists, according to Nicholas Parisi, President of the Rod Serling Memorial Foundation. Parisi's exhaustive search of archives and private collections throughout the four-year process of writing his masterful book *Rod Serling: His Life, Work, and Imagination* produced no trace of it. But Nick hasn't lost hope, nor have I, that it will turn up one day.

15 🏃

CHRISTOPHER BENEDICT

During the special broadcast by *Dr. Christian* star and award show host Jean Hersholt, Rod acknowledged during his incisive remarks that he was "fond of boxing."

ROUND 3

WKRC in Cincinnati

Rod and Carol Serling graduated from Antioch College on June 24, 1950. Shortly after, they packed up their belongings they had accumulated into the little trailer they shared and made the 70-some-odd-mile trip south from Yellow Springs to Cincinnati.

Serling joined WLW, "the nation's station," as a radio staff writer. The position involved mostly menial and unfulfilling tasks like advertising copy, local interest stories, and comedy skits for variety shows. More so than the meager pay and creative frustration, the lack of name recognition for the pieces Serling wrote particularly bothered him.

This discontent with WLW led Serling through the doors of the station's crosstown competitor, WKRC. There, he would avail himself of the station's live television anthology program *The Storm* to dive headlong into the medium for which he would soon create a tidal wave of innovation.

The Storm was the brainchild of WKRC producer and director Bob Huber, who envisioned it as a series of stand-alone mysteries. Huber, however, ultimately abandoned this somewhat limiting concept in favor of encompassing varying genres. Serling would follow suit with *The Twilight Zone*, which was advertised and sold as a science fiction/fantasy series but told its unique brand of cautionary parables through the use of war stories, westerns, post-apocalyptic horrors, time travel tales with a twist, nostalgic drama, and kooky comedies where androids, space aliens, the Devil or Death personified existed in a shared universe alongside burned-out businessmen, a bookworm with broken glasses, and boxers—both human and robot—trying to push past their stamped expiration date.

The Storm and *The Twilight Zone* shared enough of a thematic similarity that Serling would revisit—and sometimes directly rework—his WKRC scripts to figure prominently in the lore of his landmark creation. It is quite clear why Serling biographer Nicholas Parisi, while undertaking the first serious study of the crucial Cincinnati period in Serling's professional life, would draw a natural line of trajectory between the two programs.

Huber accepted thirty-one of Serling's scripts to produce on *The Storm* in a mere nine-month span between July 1951 and April 1952, replaying a pair of the shows during this time. This rapid production pace demonstrates Serling's unrelenting work ethic.

Because he was still employed by WLW at the time, the byline of Serling's first several scripts produced by WKRC bore the pen name R. Edward Sterling to avoid a potential conflict of interest. For example, WLW aired the first episode of a fifteen-minute-long sitcom Serling had developed called

"Leave it to Kathy" the night before his first script for *The Storm*, "Keeper of the Chair," was broadcast on WKRC. Pseudonym notwithstanding, Rod Serling soon began to make a name for himself.

Bob Huber was intent on selling *The Storm* to network TV. He elected to make a Kinescope recording of Serling's boxing story "Aftermath," which aired on the evening of November 27, 1951, in the hope of attracting potential buyers at CBS, future home to *The Twilight Zone*. As it happens, the Kinescope machine proved to be an unreliable ally. The picture came out clean enough, but the sound was distorted beyond comprehension and rendered the overall recording virtually useless.

The Kinescope does still exist but is not publicly accessible. More disappointing still, the script for "Aftermath" is nowhere to be found among Rod Serling's papers. There isn't even so much as a story summary available, unfortunately. Incidentally, "Aftermath" was broadcast on August 31, 1954, as a radio drama on *It Happens to You*, a program NBC had acquired from WLW.

WKRC aired a second boxing story of Serling's for *The Storm* entitled "The Twilight Rounds" on January 22, 1952. The episode itself is lost, though some B-roll footage apparently remains. "The Twilight Rounds" would also live to fight another day as an hour-long episode of NBC's *Kraft Theatre* the following year, costarring boxing legend Tony Canzoneri. Before this second rendition of "The Twilight Rounds," however, the three-division world champion would appear in another Serling-scripted boxing program for CBS: "The Face of Autumn."

***

In the wake of his graduation from Antioch College, Serling had retained the services of Blanche Gaines, a Manhattan literary agent. Gaines had agreed to shop his scripts around to radio and television producers based on her hunch that his work had merit. Like a broken record, she pleaded again and again with her Cincinnati-based client to take his talents to New York or Hollywood, "if you really want to go places."

Serling was reluctant, owing to big city insecurities. Instead, he made several brief and costly trips back and forth from Cincinnati to Manhattan to take part in story conferences and rehearsals of shows he had written that were going into production.

Purchased by CBS for their *Lux Video Theatre* series, "The Face of Autumn" would be the first of Serling's boxing stories to be transmitted to a nationwide home viewing audience on the evening of November 3,

1952. Another tragically lost broadcast that belongs to the ages, "The Face of Autumn" is summarized by Nicholas Parisi in *Rod Serling: His Life, Work, and Imagination* as the half-hour-long tale of a boxing manager whose "obsessive search for a championship contender takes a toll on his long-suffering wife."

The cast included Frank Campanella, who made his television debut three years before on *Captain Video* and *His Video Rangers* (which fans of *The Honeymooners* will recall being a favorite of Ed Norton). Ralph Kramden's idiosyncratic neighbor was played, of course, by Art Carney. Rod Serling was greatly enamored with Carney, so much so that Serling would later cast him in a *Playhouse 90* production called "The Velvet Alley" and as a drunken department store Santa in *The Twilight Zone* Christmas story "Night of the Meek." Campanella, meanwhile, landed his first film appearance over the course of a 55-year career as a detective in *Somebody Up There Likes Me*, the 1956 biopic about former middleweight champion Rocky Graziano.

The popular and immediately recognizable character actor Bill Erwin, best known for *Planes, Trains and Automobiles* and *Home Alone*, played a reporter in "The Face of Autumn," and among the staggering number of screen credits on his résumé (reportedly 241), four would take him through *The Twilight Zone* in "Mr. Denton on Doomsday," "Walking Distance," "Will the Real Martian Please Stand Up?" and "Mute."

Tony Canzoneri's character is a former champion named Packy Mendez, a role with which he just so happened to be intimately familiar. Canzoneri was the embodiment of the prototypical Serling boxer: tough as a longshoreman but tenderhearted as a schoolmarm. A fan-friendly, never-say-die fighter in the ring, Tony was generous and gregarious in equal measure, especially well-loved by the neighborhood kids who would clamor around the champ for a handshake, or an autograph, or just to be in his proximity.

Aside from their shared grim determination to succeed in their individually chosen profession, Canzoneri and Serling also both had grocers for fathers. Tony's dad ran his own store in the Italian section of New Orleans. Canzoneri realized his true calling at a young age there when he first met Pete Herman, then-current bantamweight world champion who lived a mere three blocks away from the Canzoneris. Becoming a fixture at the local gyms when he was only eleven, Tony buddied up with a journeyman lightweight fighter named Basil Galiano, who offered guidance to the scrap-happy youngster he dubbed 'The Italian Terror.'

The Canzoneri patriarch migrated to Brooklyn alone and resumed his grocery business, with the rest of the family following in his footsteps once he had firmly established himself. While in the process of racking up more than 80 amateur bouts within one year's time, Tony reacquainted himself with Galiano, who was in town training for an upcoming fight at Stillman's Gym. Canzoneri sparred three rounds with his former mentor, catching the eye of Pete Herman's manager Sammy Goldman.

With Goldman in his corner, Canzoneri made his professional debut with a first-round knockout of Jack Grodner at the Rockaway Beach Arena on July 24, 1925, and quickly rattled off a 30-fight unbeaten streak before tasting his first defeat on points to a rugged Panamanian named Davey Abad, who never wore a title belt but did manage to take one of three bouts against the pound-for-pound great Henry Armstrong.

Unsuccessful in his first two title bids, a draw with and loss to Bud Taylor for the vacant National Boxing Association bantamweight championship, Canzoneri won the unclaimed NYSAC featherweight belt in 1927 with a unanimous decision over Johnny Dundee in what was widely criticized as a lackluster affair. The same could not be said of Canzoneri's unsuccessful attempt at becoming the undisputed featherweight champion when he was matched opposite fellow titleholder Andre Routis at the Garden. *The New York Times* called it "one of the most savage fights ever staged for the 126-pound crown."

After reversing this loss to Routis in a non-title fight, Tony once again came out on the short end of a split decision against world lightweight champion Sammy Mendell at Chicago Stadium. He subsequently absorbed what the *Times* called "one of the worst beatings he has ever experienced" at the hands of Jack 'Kid' Berg. Canzoneri rebounded with a 10-fight win streak before dropping a decision to the seasoned veteran and future hall of famer Billy Petrolle. Nevertheless, he would score a shocking upset in his next bout when he knocked out the heavily favored world lightweight champion Al Singer in just a little more than one minute to win a title in his second weight class.

In Canzoneri's first defense, he would not only gain a large measure of revenge over Jack 'Kid' Berg by way of a third- round knockout but lay claim to the world junior welterweight title in the bargain, joining the exclusive club of three-division champions. Tony would floor Berg twice, once from an apparent low blow in the eighth round which went unacknowledged by the referee, in their rubber match at the Polo Grounds four and a half months later en route to a unanimous decision victory.

Eking out a split decision win over Kid Chocolate in an instant classic at Madison Square Garden in November 1931, Canzoneri left no room for debate in their rematch two years later by obliterating the Cuban sensation in the second round. At the time, some were beginning to question how much Tony, who had now been in 120 professional fights, had left in the tank.

The span of time between his bouts with Kid Chocolate was marked by both triumph and vanquishment. After allowing the unheralded Johnny Jadick to swipe his junior welterweight crown, Tony was at his absolute best the night he successfully defended his lightweight title against his former conqueror Billy Petrolle. Three weeks prior, he even had the chance to knock out Billy's brother Frankie at Ebbets Field. Canzoneri never got the opportunity to square off opposite Pete Petrolle, eldest of the three boxing siblings, and was thus denied a potential hat trick against the entire Petrolle clan.

Though there was certainly no shame in Canzoneri's hotly contested majority-decision loss to legend-in-the-making Barney Ross at Chicago Stadium on June 23, 1933, he had only himself to blame for falling short in his bid to reclaim the lightweight championship—as well as his old junior welterweight belt, now worn by Ross—after having precious points deducted for low blows in the sixth, eighth, and ninth rounds. These penalties would cost Tony dearly again in their Polo Grounds rematch, where Ross emerged with a split-decision victory.

Canzoneri kept fighting at a breakneck pace, often every month with some bouts spaced apart by a mere matter of weeks. When Barney Ross forfeited the world lightweight title, Tony was pitted against a force of nature in Lou Ambers, the 13-to-5 betting favorite, for the vacant strap at Madison Square Garden in May 1935. Grounding the 'Herkimer Hurricane' on three occasions, Canzoneri earned a unanimous decision and the lightweight title.

Ambers ended what would be Tony's last championship reign sixteen months later, awarded the fifteen-round verdict on all three judges' scorecards by relatively comfortable margins. He would give an even more impressive repeat performance in their third and final fight in May 1937, with Tony getting completely outclassed and winning just two of the fifteen rounds.

Staggered in between the trilogy with Lou Ambers were a pair of showdowns with former two-time world welterweight champion Jimmy McLarnin, who had taken the title from Young Corbett III then traded it back and forth with Barney Ross over the course of their three fights in exactly twelve months' time. This is the type of battle that boxing fans love to see. Two fierce warriors nearing the ends of their respective campaigns coming together with no specific airing of grievances to settle, no title belt on the line, simply clashing for pride's sake, relevance, bragging rights, or perhaps all three.

Canzoneri turned back the clock in their first contest, brutalizing McLarnin in a display of primal supremacy. Conversely, Tony got his clock cleaned when they resumed hostilities four and a half months later, with the baby-faced Irishman beating him to a pulp.

Your average person's early thirties can often be looked upon as their peak years. Not necessarily so with boxers. Especially ones who, like Canzoneri, had subjected their bodies and brains to inconceivable punishment throughout who knew how many rounds in more than 170 fights. And that's not counting the sparring, the roadwork, and the hours that defy calculation spent skipping rope, doing pushups and sit-ups, whaling away at the heavy bag in the gym, and starving oneself to the brink of exhaustion and dehydration to make weight for the next fight.

There is an emotional price to pay as well. The time commitment required by the profession forces a fighter to become, by necessity, a largely absentee husband and father (wife and mother for female boxers) while taking as many bouts as their manager can secure in as short a period of time as possible to put bread on the table and butter it too.

A ghost of his former fighting self, Canzoneri soldiered on until November 1, 1939, when he suffered his first and only stoppage loss. Al 'Bummy' Davis sent Tony twice to the canvas on his way to a barbaric third-round TKO. The fans assembled inside the Garden, nearly every single one a Canzoneri loyalist, booed Davis and never forgave him for beating up on their beloved local hero.

A well-remembered and happily retired Canzoneri tallied up an astonishing professional record of 137-24-10 and would be posthumously honored among the immortals enshrined in the International Boxing Hall of Fame as part of its inaugural Class of 1990. The late, great, cigar-chomping, fedora-wearing boxing scribe Bert Randolph Sugar ranked Canzoneri at number nine—one spot above Muhammad Ali, mind you—in his 1984 book *The 100 Greatest Boxers of All Time*, praising Tony as "a shooting star of unforgettable magnitude."

He was only fifty-one when he was found dead on the bed in his room at the Hotel Bryant with no sign of struggle or foul play. The boxing gods, it seems, had simply come to claim another sacrificial lamb before his time should have rightfully been up. Sounding like a character straight out of a Rod Serling story, Canzoneri insisted that every drop of blood and every stitch used to close up every wound had all been worth it.

***

Tony Canzoneri began his foray into show business while still an active boxer. He appeared with fellow prizefighters Jack Dempsey, Primo Carnera, and 'Slapsie' Maxie Rosenbloom in the feature film variety showcase *Mr. Broadway*, hosted by Ed Sullivan, in 1933. Two years later, he scored a bit part in a romantic comedy called *Let's Live Tonight*. After hanging up the gloves, Tony was given small roles in the 1949 boxing drama *Ringside* and John Ford's *Stagecoach* starring John Wayne. Canzoneri followed these film appearances with Rod Serling's "The Face of Autumn," which, in turn, would lead him to be cast in another boxing-themed program written by Serling.

As discussed earlier, "The Twilight Rounds" had previously aired on WKRC's *The Storm* as a half-hour televised drama. It was reworked and doubled in length when it was picked up by NBC for its *Kraft Theatre* anthology series and broadcast on May 27, 1953. Canzoneri portrayed a minor character named, naturally enough, Tony. The rest of the cast is rich with future *Twilight Zone* alums.

In "The Twilight Rounds," Serling tells the story of middleweight contender Scotty Beckitt, played in the episode by Frank Maxwell, who would resurface in *The Twilight Zone* seven years later as movie director Marty Fisher in "A World of Difference." Intent on overturning the hourglass and making one final and unlikely run at a title shot, 34-year-old Scotty is deliberately deaf to the pleas of his kindhearted manager Googy to walk away from boxing while he is still literally able to.

If you recall, Googy was also the name of the manager in Serling's 1948 short story "The Good Right Hard." This isn't meant to imply that he is the same individual, as Serling had a penchant for reusing character names throughout his various works. It is interesting to note that *A Streetcar Named Desire* and *On the Waterfront* director Elia Kazan portrayed a hoodlum named Googi (different spelling) in the 1940 boxing movie *City*

For Conquest starring James Cagney. We'll never know for sure, but perhaps Serling saw the film and became enamored by the unusual name of Kazan's character.

This version of Googy was played by J. Pat O'Malley, your typical "hard-working actor of the day," to borrow a phrase from *The Twilight Zone Podcast* host Tom Elliot. *Twilight Zone* fans remember him best as Old Ben from "The Fugitive," but he put in three additional appearances in the fifth dimension: as Homburg in "The Chaser," the old man in the hospital bed in "The Self-Improvement of Salvadore Ross," and Gooberman the town drunk in "Mr. Garrity and the Graves."

Googy illustrates his point to the obstinate Scotty by using a good-natured but badly damaged ex-boxer named Max who works at the gym as a walking, talking cautionary tale. Maxie, played by Mike Kellin (who would also subsequently find himself in *The Twilight Zone* by way of "The Thirty-Fathom Grave") has a life-threatening brain embolism to show for his hard-fought efforts in the ring. He also exhibits the telltale signs of what would later be scientifically classified as dementia pugilistica and is now known as CTE, or Chronic Traumatic Encephalopathy.

Put another way, Max is "punch drunk," which was the uncharitable nomenclature assigned to the condition at the time. He brags to anyone who will listen about the night he lasted the full distance with the legendary Sugar Ray Robinson, blissfully unaware that he's told them the same story a hundred times before.

Besides blind ambition, one of the main reasons for Scotty overstaying his welcome in the fight game is his fiancée Margie, a gold-digging former lounge singer who negates Googy's protests as well as the honest assessment of his promoter Nick (Carlos Montalbán, who was also in *The Harder They Fall*) that he "ain't got it anymore," by issuing self-serving demands for Scotty to not be "yellow" and chase after a shot at the middleweight championship.

To this end, Googy appeals to Scotty to not only retire from boxing but to leave Margie behind as well, which he feels will force his fighter to finally deal with the situation in a more reasonable manner. Barbara Baxley was cast in the role of Marge, and she would not only costar in the fourth season *Twilight Zone* episode "Mute" as the foster mother of a young Ann Jillian but also appeared in the 1980s revival as Dr. Kate Wange in a segment entitled "Profile in Silver" (1986).

In a petty and passive-aggressive display of her influence over Scotty, Marge instructs Scotty to work over his sparring partner with needless hostility, earning Googy's utter disdain. No longer able to bite his tongue, Googy confronts Scotty in the dressing room before his next fight and bad-mouths Marge, resulting in a lethal chain of events. Scotty punches Googy, and Max instinctively enters the fray even though being struck in the head is very liable to kill him.

Scotty initially cools off enough to realize this and stands down until Margie throws in her two cents, insisting that he defend himself. Like a dutiful lapdog obeying its master's command, Scotty lays Maxie out with a single blow. Max is taken away in an ambulance and dies in the hospital later that night. A fabricated story about Maxie suffering his fatal head injury in an accidental fall saves Scotty from prosecution. With his ties to Googy now severed, he is left with only Marge, for whom he promises to carry forward and win the title.

Two years after the fact, Scotty is matched opposite Andy Pinella, Googy's latest protégé, and asks his former mentor to have his younger and stronger contender "go slow" during their bout. Scotty goes so far as to suggest that Pinella take a dive, with his rationale being that Andy's budding career can easily withstand this small bump in the road whereas Scotty has one final shot at achieving boxing immortality.

Although he appears sympathetic to Scotty's pleas, Googy uses his intimate knowledge of his former fighter's vulnerabilities to instruct Pinella how to exploit them and "teach him a lesson" in the process. Indeed, Scotty is knocked out in the eleventh round of a hellacious slugfest. Badly battered, he knows that the time has come for him to hang up the gloves for good.

He confesses to Googy in the dressing room that Margie never even showed up to the arena and assumes that she will have nothing more to do with him after that night. Googy assures him that he should feel no shame, and Scotty can't help but take one final walk to the ring where he studies the vacant seats, quietly reflecting on the past and contemplating what the future might look like.

ROUND

4

Television's Angry Young Man

Rod Serling estimated that pretty much every script of his bought by the major networks between 1952 and 1953 had been "noncontroversial" and "socially inoffensive." This was something he knew had to change. And it would, albeit probably not soon enough for his liking.

In a concession to upward mobility, Rod and Carol Serling moved to Westport, Connecticut with their firstborn daughter Jodi in the latter part of 1954. This living situation represented the best of both worlds, allowing Serling to largely retain the small-town sensibilities he cherished so dearly while being able to reach New York City and the necessary evil of its hustling and bustling boardrooms in just a little over an hour.

While on the topic of career advancement and corporate America, Serling's teleplay "Patterns" would prove to be a game changer for the frustrated writer. Airing live on NBC's *Kraft Television Theatre* the evening of January 12, 1955, and starring Richard Kiley, Everett Sloane, Ed Begley, and Elizabeth Montgomery, "Patterns" was an impassioned, scathing indictment of the way commercial enterprise can crush the soul of a virtuous man, its ruthless machinery slowly but relentlessly grinding down his will to live.

To say that "Patterns" was well-received would be a strenuous exercise in understatement. Addressing his "overnight success" two years later, Serling commented that his phone started ringing no sooner than "Patterns" had gone off the air and hadn't stopped since.

In an unprecedented move to satisfy public demand, NBC reassembled the cast and crew on February 9th to broadcast an encore performance. "Patterns" earned Serling his first Emmy award. It garnered enough acclaim to warrant a motion picture adaptation of his teleplay the following year, with Van Heflin inheriting the lead role of Fred Staples from Richard Kiley.

No longer was Rod Serling flying under the radar. Staying aloft in rarefied air, however, would be a struggle unto itself, one which would see Serling join the ranks of television's angry young men in the company of Paddy Chayefsky, Reginald Rose, Horton Foote, and Robert Alan Arthur.

Richard Grossman was an editor at Simon and Schuster who assisted Serling with the 1957 publication of *Patterns*, which compiled the titular teleplay along with "The Rack," "Old MacDonald Had a Curve," and "Requiem for a Heavyweight" in one volume. An astute observer, Grossman had boxed in college and drew a direct parallel between Serling's intensity and that of the prizefighter, saying that "his eyes moved like a boxer's."

CBS programmer Mike Dann concurred with Grossman's assessment. Whenever a perturbed Serling gravely locked eyes with someone, Dann recounted, "you knew you were in trouble."

***

Courtesy of *Ford Television Theatre*, which had migrated from CBS to NBC in 1951, "Garrity's Sons" was Serling's first post-"Patterns" boxing story to be transmitted over the airwaves. Directed by thirteen-time *Ford Television Theatre* contributor Fred F. Sears, "Garrity's Sons" was broadcast on March 24, 1955, while Serling was still the toast of the town. The story opens in a gym as trainer Rory Garrity calls "time!" to signal the end of his newest fighter Chick Charleston's sparring session.

Chick is played by Abel Fernandez, who would go on to score a role as a series regular on *The Untouchables* television show as Agent William Longfellow, while Rory was portrayed by, well, Rory Calhoun. He featured in 1945's *The Great John L.* as James J. Corbett, the first fighter to win the heavyweight championship under the newly adopted Marquess of Queensberry rules by beating John L. Sullivan in 1892, and he starred as a sparring partner to George Tony Angelo in *Nob Hill* the very next month. Calhoun would also have a major part to play in Serling's next boxing project, "Champion." But let's not get ahead of ourselves.

Rory sends Chick to the showers and immediately becomes incensed at an onlooker's favorable comparison between Charleston and Rory's estranged kid brother Steve, a top-rated light-heavyweight whom he used to train. Rory insists that Steve could have knocked Chick out with one arm. Before he can get to the locker room, Rory is stopped yet again. A manager is looking for a trainer who can grant an aging perennial heavyweight contender named Sammy a stay of execution in the fight racket.

An indignant Rory suggests instead that the manager "take him to a good doctor and have his head examined." To knock Rory off his high horse, the manager reminds him that Steve was one of the dirtiest fighters in the business. This comment only infuriates Rory further. He finishes his rude brush-off of the pair by turning his misdirected anger on Sammy. Rory declares that he wants to see Sammy no closer to a boxing ring than eating popcorn in the third row before literally and figuratively slamming the door on the conversation.

Sammy's role in "Garrity's Sons" may end there, but the man who portrayed him would return in Serling's future work. Charles Horvath was another "hardworking actor of the day" (with a wink and a nod to Tom Elliot of *The Twilight Zone Podcast*) and will warrant further discussion when covering *The Twilight Zone's* boxing episodes. Horvath appeared in "The

Big, Tall Wish" as Bolie Jackson's opponent, Joey Consiglio. But again, first things first.

Back in the locker room, Rory attempts to convince Chick, who has only three bouts—all wins—on his professional record, to walk away from boxing, "without weaving" he adds. Chick wants no part of being assigned the reputation of a quitter. Rory reminds him that Gene Tunney quit the boxing business, and no one had the guts to call him names to his face. Chick good-naturedly points out that Tunney retired as a champion and that they can pick up this subject again when he himself has a title. Sensing the motivation behind Rory's request, Chick intuitively but gently responds that "they don't all turn out like Steve."

Rory opens up to Chick regarding his brother who, he confesses, went from being as contrite as a professional fighter can be, holding out his gloves apologetically toward an opponent at any perceived infraction on his part, to a back-handing heel within two years.

Rory comes home to find out from his father (James Bell, from producer Val Lewton's classic 1940s chillers *I Walked with a Zombie* and *The Leopard Man*) that Steve, who has been staging a comeback and boxing out of Pittsburgh, will be arriving shortly thanks to the train fare that their forgiving-to-a-fault Pop sent him.

Trying to make the old man see the error of his ways, Rory shouts at Pop that there are only a few things his precious Steve cares about and is good at—fighting dirty, finding cheap booze, and even cheaper women. He harshly offers to pay for Steve's train fare home himself, but only if it's to transport his dead body back after it has been picked up out of an alley.

Played by May Wynn (*The Caine Mutiny*), Peggy enters the room as Rory and Pop engage in their verbal tug-of-war. We soon learn that Peggy has been romantically involved with both Garrity boys. Steve was her childhood crush and first love until they got serious. He then became abusive and skipped town, whereupon she presumably turned to Rory for emotional support, which led to their current engagement.

Peg has made a series of flimsy excuses to put off their wedding, but Rory knows she still carries a flame for his no-good little brother. As wrong as she knows her impulses to be, she holds out some hope that Steve can once again become the "guy with a dream" she fell for in the first place.

The tension is ratcheted up when the prodigal son returns, much to the delight of his father and the annoyance of his brother. Steve (played by Vince Edwards, of later *Ben Casey* fame) asks Rory to train him for a run at

33

the title, but his brother reminds him of the fact that he walked out on their contract so that he could be represented by a mob-controlled syndicate instead.

Rory also rubs it in Steve's face that their father's devotion to him is non-reciprocal, evidenced by his absence during Pop's serious illness because he was holed up with "one of your bargain basement babes and a couple of bottles." Rory could forgive all of that, but not what Steve did to Peggy. Incidentally, Steve is portrayed by Vince Edwards, who would later star in the title role of the *Ben Casey* television series from 1961-66.

When Pop fetches her, Peggy almost immediately becomes locked in an amorous embrace with Steve, who then proceeds to lay Rory out with a short left hook to the liver and another to the jaw after being called "a dirty, lousy crumb-bum." It's Rory, however, who gets in the parting shot by admonishing Steve for his inability to use a problem-solving method that doesn't involve his fists. Before exiting the room, he cautions Pop and Peg not to get any of the dirt covering Steve on them.

A newspaper headline reports that the Garrity brothers will be in opposite corners when Steve is matched against Rory's fighter, Chick Charleston. Conventional wisdom predicts that this is a 50/50 fight, with Chick being younger and hungrier but Steve enjoying the advantage in experience and underhanded tactics.

Peg tells Rory that her relationship with Steve stands a chance only if he loses the bout against Chick so that he can bow out of the fight game on his own terms and take the job that her boss has offered him. If he wins, Peggy insists that it's over between them. Rory, however, isn't buying it for a second. He knows all too well that she is stuck on him whatever transpires. She asks whether Rory can find his way to forgiving his brother. His response is cold, succinct, and negative.

Visiting Rory in his office at the gym, Steve inquires as to how good a fighter Chick is and then begs to have him take a dive. The circumstances mirror Scotty Beckitt's request of his former manager Googy prior to his bout against the hot prospect Andy Pinella in "The Twilight Rounds." Same as Scotty did, Steve impresses upon his brother the importance of him looking good in this fight with the window of opportunity closing rapidly.

Steve's admission of guilt regarding past transgressions seems sincere, as he breaks down his primal mindset for Rory in easy-to-understand terminology, confessing that punching, hitting, and bleeding were all he knew. He switches gears, assuring Rory that he will attempt to win the fight on his own merit, but asks that he instruct Chick to focus his attack on head shots rather than body blows, to which he is particularly susceptible.

Rory sends Steve away with the promise that he will think about it. In the locker room on the night of the fight, however, he specifically informs Chick about his brother's vulnerable midsection and tells him to hurt Steve bad as a personal favor. Sure enough, as the action picks up in the third round, Chick works Steve's body over and then comes back upstairs with a right cross, flooring him.

Steve regains his footing, but not for long. Chick continues an ambidextrous assault against Steve's body before dislodging his mouthpiece with a left hook that sends him slumping to the canvas yet again. The bout is mercifully halted in the next round.

The denouement of "Garrity's Sons" takes place where we started, back in the gym where a solemn, busted-up Steve knew he would find Rory after the fight is over. He confesses not only that he is washed up but that Peggy had come clean about her talk with Rory. He understands, and is thankful for, why events played out as they did, ultimately for his own good.

Rory tells Steve he wishes he could have taken the beating for him. Aware of how visibly Rory is losing a wrestling match with his emotions, Steve replies that it looks like he did. The two Garrity boys stroll off with their arms around one another's shoulders and head home for what Peggy calls a victory party.

***

With television enjoying its Golden Age, the number of U.S. households boasting at least one set skyrocketed from less than 10,000 in 1945 to nearly 60 million by the end of the 50s. Anthology programs became exceedingly popular, offering the rapidly multiplying number of viewers original programming as well as unique takes on familiar source material. They gave a rotating cast of actors, directors, and writer opportunities to test their mettle in a variety of genres.

Rod Serling made the most of this opportunity as often as humanly possible. It took only one week to the day from the airing of "Garrity's Sons" for his follow-up boxing-themed story to be broadcast on network TV.

Shown on CBS' *Climax!* series at 8:30 pm the evening of March 31, 1955, "The Champion" was Serling's adaptation of the short story by revered sports columnist and humorist Ring Lardner, who is probably best known for his 1916 baseball novel *You Know Me Al*. Published that same year in *Metropolitan* magazine, "Champion" tells the tale of an unscrupulous prizefighter named Midge Kelly.

Serling's dramatized version of Lardner's story was, of course, not the first. His was preceded by the 1949 feature film, with a script from Carl Foreman, who would soon after win great acclaim for *High Noon* but feel the wrath of the Hollywood blacklist. In the movie Midge was portrayed by relative newcomer and first-time Academy Award nominee Kirk Douglas. The 1950 statuette was taken home instead by Lon Chaney Jr.'s old drinking buddy Broderick Crawford for *All the King's Men*. Interestingly, the *Twilight Zone* classic "To Serve Man" features a stock footage sequence of Times Square with a billboard advertising Kirk Douglas' *Champion* visible in the background.

Fresh from his starring turn in "Garrity's Sons," Rory Calhoun returned to assume the role of Midge Kelly in Serling's "The Champion." While he is training for his upcoming heavyweight title defense against top contender Jack Riley, Midge's life story is told through a series of flashbacks during an interview given to a newspaperman by his manager Jerome Harris (Ray Collins, who played Orson Welles' gubernatorial opponent Jim W. Gettys in *Citizen Kane*). Harris feeds the reporter a heaping helping of baloney, making Midge out to be more virtuous than a choirboy. The truth of the matter, however, is soon revealed. The journalist is played by John Craven, who would later be featured in the Serling-scripted *Twilight Zone* cautionary tale "The Old Man in the Cave" as well as a sheriff in one episode of Rod's short-lived western series, *The Loner*, which was titled "The Ordeal of Bud Windom."

Midge's upbringing was anything but ideal. As a young boy, he lived in a run-down tenement on the south side of Chicago with his little brother Connie and their tormentor of a father. An inebriate and ne'er do well, the Kelly patriarch by the name of Bunko was played by popular character actor Wallace Ford. Ford specialized in fast-talking, wisecracking fellas like the ones he personified in such varied fare as Tod Browning's controversial 1932 sideshow film *Freaks*, a pair of Universal *Mummy* sequels, the fantastic 1949 pugilistic film noir *The Set-Up*, Hitchcock's *Spellbound*, *Harvey* with Jimmy Stewart, and *The Great John L.*

While Lardner cast Midge Kelly as an irredeemable scoundrel from the outset of his story, Serling's narrative takes an interesting detour. He opts to instead reconcile the cruelty exhibited by the motherless Midge by suggesting that the fighter is merely repeating the cycle of terrible behavior learned from his father.

Lardner's story begins with seventeen-year-old Midge, whose real name is Michael, knocking his crippled brother Connie out of his wheel-chair for the half-dollar he's holding and, conceivably, just for the fun of it. When their mother Ellen returns home from her shift at Faulkner's Steam Laundry and discovers Connie lying on the floor, she confronts Midge, who unconscionably punches her as well.

Curiously, there is no father present in Lardner's story, and Serling again goes the opposite direction by omitting Ellen Kelly from his teleplay. Furthermore, while we are left to assume in Lardner's story that Connie's condition is most likely the result of an illness or birth defect, Rod includes in his script a sequence where Connie suffers debilitating injuries in a fall from their second-story apartment window while attempting to flee from one of Bunko's drunken, abusive outbursts.

After he becomes a boxer, Midge quickly finds that the paltry purse money earned from winning prelim bouts pales in comparison to the amounts of cash pressed into his palm for throwing fights, earning a spotty record and checkered reputation along the way. An association with manager Tommy Haley brings Midge some much needed legitimacy, accompanied by a full-on sprint toward the world title.

Haley is played by Wally Brown, who in the recent past had been half of a comedy duo with Alan Carney. A sort of poor man's Abbott and Costello, Brown and Carney beat that farcical pair to the punch in terms of playing opposite Bela Lugosi by appearing in two late-40s RKO flicks with the once and future Count Dracula called *Zombies* on Broadway and *Genius at Work*. Both were light on the horror and debatably heavy on the humor.

No sooner does Midge attain the championship than he leaves his loyal manager in the lurch and cozies up to the wife of Haley's replacement. Serling evidently made yet another alteration to Ring Lardner's short story, in which a character named Lou Hersch was a fight fan who befriends Midge and introduces the boxer to his sister Emma, fated to become the neglected Mrs. Kelly. In Serling's iteration, Lou Hersch apparently becomes Midge's second manager and Emma is now Lou's wife, with whom Midge runs off after winning the heavyweight title.

Emma is portrayed in Serling's "The Champion" by Geraldine Brooks, an admirer of Katherine Hepburn who transitioned from the Broadway stage to the big screen. She debuted in the 1947 film noir *Possessed* alongside Joan Crawford, Van Heflin, and Raymond Massey. From there, she would guest star on TV shows like *Bonanza*, *The Fugitive*, *Gunsmoke*, and two episodes of *The Outer Limits*, among others.

37

Shortly after her divorce from television writer Herbert Sargent (*The Tonight Show Starring Johnny Carson, Saturday Night Live*), Brooks married novelist and screenwriter Budd Schulberg. His incendiary 1947 boxing book *The Harder They Fall* (featuring a character named Toro Molina, who was a thinly veiled caricature of former heavyweight champion Primo Carnera) was adapted nine years later into a film starring Humphrey Bogart in his last role.

Schulberg also composed the screenplay for 1954's *On the Waterfront* (in addition to the subsequent novel, simply titled *Waterfront*) which features Marlon Brando as a longshoreman and ex-boxer named Terry Malloy who memorably laments to his mobbed-up brother Charley, played by Rod Steiger, that "I coulda been a contender."

Featuring Budd's writing and Geraldine's photographs, Brooks and Schulberg collaborated on a 1975 book entitled *Swan Watch*, which chronicled the interactions they shared with their hissing, feathered friends Loh and Grin on the shore of Long Island Sound abutting the couple's property in Quogue.

Unfortunately, Brooks passed away two years later at the age of 51 from complications of cancer. Schulberg wasted little time remarrying, his fourth and final union, and was 95 when he died in 2009. At the time he was hard at work on a script for a Joe Louis biopic which would have been directed by Spike Lee, as Budd told me not long before his passing.

Anger and rage are typically huge liabilities for a fighter during a bout, as they cloud one's judgment and thus impair the ability to think logically and act accordingly. Midge Kelly, however, uses them as primary tools of the trade. They've gotten him all the way to the world title, so why shouldn't he trust them to work in his favor against challenger Jack Riley?

Former heavyweight boxer Tommy Garland was selected to fill the role of Jack Riley. Originally from Newfoundland, Canada, Garland relocated to Culver City, California, which allowed him to conveniently pull double duty as an actor in Hollywood and a prizefighter primarily in and around Santa Monica. Albeit against opposition of an unspectacular nature and with no shot at even a regional title to show for it, Garland accumulated a pretty impressive 45-14-5 record and had the distinction of never having been knocked out. His film résumé boasts appearances in no less than eleven boxing movies from his debut in 1939's *Golden Boy* to *The Harder They Fall* and *Somebody Up There Likes Me*, both released in 1956.

Cruising to victory over Riley, Midge becomes distracted by the sight of his brother Connie's crutch propped up against his ringside seat, which seems to stir up spontaneous feelings of remorse. Consequently, Midge is caught unawares and rendered defenseless, beaten so badly that he needs to be removed from the ring on a stretcher. His championship is not all he would forfeit. Midge dies from his injuries soon after he is conveyed to the dressing room.

Connie, played by character actor Tommy Cook, asks everyone gathered around the dressing room table, "Won't someone cry for him?" Tellingly, no one can or will shed a tear. No one, that is, except for a now sober and repentant Bunko Kelly, who learns of his son's death in the newspaper.

The fate assigned to Midge Kelly in Rod Serling's teleplay is another radical departure from Ring Lardner's text, in which the conclusion is left open-ended and unresolved. It terminates instead with the publication of the sportswriter's misguided puff piece on the still very much alive boxer. Serling's ending is also consistent with the type of cosmic justice that would be subsequently meted out in *The Twilight Zone*, where individuals found guilty of moral bankruptcy in a trial by fire got their comeuppance in one unique way or another.

***

Rod Serling was, without question, fueled by a compulsive inner drive to become a writer of consequence and renown, and "Patterns" was one giant step in the right direction. If the teleplay itself was any indication, however, Serling strongly disapproved of the succeed-at-all-costs mentality, especially when it came in the form of climbing the ladder by stepping on the backs of others. This he had no tolerance for. He was determined to get ahead by keeping a stiff upper lip and diligently honing his craft, hammering out more scripts than the networks knew what to do with.

This hell bent for leather work ethic surely resonates within anyone who has ever undertaken an artistic or athletic endeavor and seen it through with the steadfast accompaniment of unbridled enthusiasm and gut-twisting anxiety. In relation to our ongoing discussion, these principles apply equally to the prizefighter as to the writer.

Serling also knew all too well that show business is a fickle mistress. He would have to summon the muses to conjure up something to rival—or hopefully surpass—the sensation he caused with "Patterns." The boxing gods would answer the bell, and that something special would materialize the following year in the guise of a story called "Requiem for a Heavyweight."

ROUND 5

Playhouse 90: Requiem for a Heavyweight (1956)

Rod Serling had a vested interest in the 8th annual Emmy Awards ceremony on the evening of March 17, 1956. Nominated for his version of Ring Lardner's "Champion" in the Best Television Adaptation category, Serling would lose out to Paul Gregory and future *Planet of the Apes* director Franklin J. Schaffner, who cowrote *The Caine Mutiny Court Martial*, based on the Pulitzer Prize- winning novel by Herman Wouk.

"Patterns," however, won for Best Original Teleplay Writing. Serling took home the first of what would eventually total six gold statuettes, an individual record which has stood the test of time.

He was bothered by the thought of being known as a one-hit wonder, the potential for which had burrowed beneath his skin and become an irritant that wouldn't go away. Seven months after the Emmys, what may have seemed like an eternity to Serling, *Playhouse 90* broadcast his story of a used-up palooka named Harlan 'Mountain' McClintock, who struggles with navigating his way through the unforgiving terrain known as life beyond the ring ropes. Jack Palance gives an unquestionably stellar performance as Mountain. As we'll cover much more later, it is very possible that his past boxing experience substantially informed his authentic portrayal.

Retrospectively scanning the horizon of his entire body of work from one end of the vista to the other, Rod Serling would later remark that "Requiem for a Heavyweight" was "as honest a piece as I've ever done." For someone with his self-effacing humility, that was high praise indeed. Hard-fought and well-deserved at that.

It was of the utmost importance to him to steer clear of the commonplace clichés depicted in certain boxing dramatizations that seemed to paint in broad brushstrokes. Serling concerned himself instead with the finer nuances of character portrayal, which would slowly strip away the layers of what you thought you already knew in an earnest journey to get to the heart of the matter.

There was much awe and wonder, and probably more than a few moist eyes, among the viewers who tuned in to *Playhouse 90* on October 11, 1956. Serling could rest assured that "Requiem for a Heavyweight" inspired none of the unintentional laughter he dreaded.

Rod Serling wrote that he always liked fighting and fighters in the Author's Commentary for his published teleplay of "Requiem for a Heavyweight," included in the 1957 collection, *Patterns*. "Requiem" would significantly up the ante from the seven previous boxing stories Serling had crafted by delving into the corrupt nature of the sport, with specific attention paid to how such malfeasance can wreak havoc on the psyche of a has-been prizefighter coping with betrayal, wounded pride, and a dubious future.

***

Director Ralph Nelson's establishing shot tracks nearer to the front door of a small arena above which hangs a banner boasting FITE TO-NIGHT. As the camera meanders through the lobby, littered with what appears to be napkins, betting slips, and discarded bout sheets, we hear the volume of the cheering crowd slowly increase and get a good look at a poster advertising the evening's ten-round main event between Mountain McClintock and Jack Gibbons.

As soon as the corridor leading to the ringside area comes into view, the off-camera announcer gives the result of a technical knockout victory in favor of Jack Gibbons at 2:14 of the seventh round. The winner comes bounding down the ramp in the company of celebratory hangers-on basking in his reflected glory, no matter how temporary.

Although his cameo is very brief, Jack Gibbons was played by John Lee Storey, better known among fight aficionados as Young Jack Johnson. With a ring moniker inspired by the first Black man to win the world heavyweight title, Johnson had been a boxing champion in the Army before turning pro and earning impressive victories over Zora Folley and Ezzard Charles.

He subsequently fell under the influence of mob boss Frank 'Blinky' Palermo, who secretly bought Johnson's contract from his manager Bert Lewis. Johnson had a consistently inconsistent career, defeating one other heavyweight notable, Willi Besmanoff, but losing to other top-rated contenders such as Eddie Machen, Karl Mildenberger, Brian London, and, on two occasions, Ernie Terrell. At the age of 35, John Lee Story, aka Young Jack Johnson, was stabbed to death by his stepdaughter Bobby Steptoe, seven months after being knocked out by Cleveland Williams.

When the winner and glad handers clear out, the barely lucid form of Mountain McClintock is dragged down the hall by his trainer Army and manager Maish, portrayed by real-life father and son Ed and Keenan Wynn, respectively. There were grave doubts expressed by many involved in the production as to how competently Ed Wynn, famous for his zany brand of comedy, would be able to pull off a serious role with lines to memorize and marks to hit, and on live television no less.

This conundrum, which thankfully proved to be unfounded as Ed Wynn turned in a wonderful, Emmy-nominated performance as Army, would serve as the subject matter for 1960's "The Man in the Funny Suit," a *Desilu Playhouse* dramatization of the making of "Requiem for a Heavyweight." It was helmed by "Requiem" director Ralph Nelson and featured Ed and Keenan Wynn playing themselves. Nelson had a small role as himself in "The Man in the Funny Suit," as did boxer Maxie Rosenbloom and none other than Rod Serling.

Ed and Keenan Wynn would both pay separate visits to *The Twilight Zone*. Ed would pass through the fifth dimension on two occasions, in "One for the Angels" and "Ninety Years Without Slumbering," and Keenan starred in the Season One finale "A World of His Own," which was also directed by Ralph Nelson and features a memorable cameo by Rod Serling at the show's conclusion. This marked the first time the series' creator appeared on camera during an actual episode of *The Twilight Zone*. All of Serling's narrations up to that point were done off-screen, and his visual presence existed only by way of his teaser for next week's offering. That would change beginning with season two, and Serling's introductions were often filmed, schedule permitting, on the episode's actual set. Otherwise, a comparable mockup was sometimes substituted.

Army is forced to haul Mountain back to the dressing room on his own when Maish is detained by a sharp-dressed, intense-looking fellow who shakes him down for money he owes to a mobster named Mr. Henson. The New York State Athletic Commission's doctor, whose thirty-eight-year career is coming to a close, enters to dress Mountain's wounds and conduct a rudimentary post-fight physical. Detecting what he calls sclerotic damage to the boxer's left pupil, a tear which is the warning sign of a detached retina and potential blindness, the physician relays to Maish that he won't be the only one retiring.

The doctor is portrayed by Edgar Stehli, who *Twilight Zone* fans will recall as Sam Kittridge in "Long Live Walter Jameson," the elderly professor who becomes wise to the fact that the title character, played by Kevin McCarthy (*Invasion of the Body Snatchers*), just might be the beneficiary of an unnatural lifespan. Prior to "Requiem," Stehli had appeared in two other Serling-penned presentations: "The Arena" for *Studio One* and "Noon on Doomsday" for *The United States Steel Hour*.

Unlike Army, Maish is less than sympathetic. Within minutes of Mountain regaining consciousness, complaining of how badly his head hurts and that his eye feels "kind of funny," Maish begins plotting to find a replacement for the tenderized piece of meat currently standing beneath a torrent

45

of hot water, cleansing himself of dried blood and regret. Rejuvenated by the shower, Mountain comes out laughing and shadow boxing. His legs are still unsteady, however, and the laughter ends abruptly when Maish informs him of the doctor's orders for him to retire.

"What'll I do?" asks Mountain pathetically. Unless you count the ability to simultaneously dish out and take a beating, he has no marketable skillset. He doubts if anyone back home in Tennessee will remember him, or he them, following a fourteen-year absence. Mountain pleads with Maish to let him try his luck getting cleared to box in another state or at least take part in club fights, all to no avail.

It's only when Mountain apologizes in all sincerity for losing that night's fight that Maish's anger dissipates and is replaced by something resembling genuine sympathy for the man he has overseen for fourteen years. For a moment, anyway. Out in the lobby, Maish and Army engage in a quick conversation with Mr. Pirelli, a wresting promoter with a hot dog in each hand and a voice that sounds as if he is gargling a throatful of gravel. Pirelli, who will reenter the story in an impactful way a little later, is played by future two-time *Twilight Zone* visitor Stanley Adams who was Buster Keaton's foil, Rollo, in "Once Upon a Time" and Jensen the bartender in "Mr. Garrity and the Graves."

The scene shifts to a hotel bar, a spot popular with ex-boxers that Maish refers to as "the graveyard" on account of the way that, as Mountain tells it, "these guys spend their time dying in here, fighting their lives away inside their heads." One-time undisputed light-heavyweight champion of the world Maxie Rosenbloom is the pug with the fedora and flattened nose holding court, regaling the congregation of former fighters circled around him with an animated play-by-play of an evening in the ring that didn't turn out too well for him when he ducked under two lefts thrown by his opponent but failed to get out of harm's way a third time.

Dating back to 1923, 'Slapsie Maxie' (a nickname bestowed onto him by famed journalist Damon Runyon due to Rosenbloom's chummy demeanor and open-handed style of boxing) was a veteran of no fewer than 272 professional prizefights, winning 207 of them. These statistics are nothing short of staggering, inconceivable by today's understandably precautionary standards.

Even before Maxie hung up the mitts for good in 1939, he began to make a decent living as an actor with almost 80 credits to his name in everything from *The Boogey Man Will Get You* with Boris Karloff and Peter

Lorre to *Abbot and Costello Meet the Keystone Kops*, *The Munsters*, *I Dream of Jeannie*, and, as middleweight legend Stanley Ketchel, in *Irish Eyes Are Smiling*.

Rosenbloom shared film sets, television studios, and nightclub stages on multiple occasions with Max Baer, who can be easily picked out of the lineup of palookas egging Maxie on in "Requiem." Among them was actor Frank Richards, later to appear in the *Twilight Zone* episode "Mr. Dingle, the Strong" featuring Burgess Meredith.

One of the revolving-door heavyweight champions of the early 1930s, Max Baer won the title from Primo Carnera in a sorry state of affairs that resembled a mid-card wrestling match rather than a heavyweight championship bout. He promptly lost it to 'Cinderella Man' Jim Braddock almost exactly one year later to the day.

Bewitched by Hollywood's siren song in 1933, Max's showbiz career began with *The Prizefighter and the Lady*. The lady in question was the beautiful Myrna Loy in the company of three prizefighters, with Baer challenging his future ring nemesis Primo Carnera in a bout promoted and refereed by Jack Dempsey.

Baer was responsible for one ring fatality, that of Frankie Campbell in 1930, and indirectly linked to another. Ernie Schaaf complained of severe headaches after being pounded to the canvas and saved by the bell in the last round of his 1932 rematch with Baer and died four days after getting knocked out by Primo Carnera less than six months later. With Baer playing what is essentially a fictionalized version of himself and actor Mike Lane portraying Toro Moreno, the mob-manufactured boxer based on Carnera, a retelling of this tragedy is depicted in *The Harder They Fall*, which was released five months before the broadcast of "Requiem."

Army and Mountain are seated at the bar where they drink a toast to his 111 fights. Ned Glass, another one of those "hardworking actors of the day," is featured as the bartender. Glass' extensive résumé contains a pair of *Twilight Zone* appearances, as the refrigerator repairman in "The Midnight Sun" and the pawnbroker in "A Passage for Trumpet," in addition to a guest spot on Rod Serling's *Night Gallery* in a segment entitled "Operation Bingo." Glass was also Ed Wynn's understudy on "Requiem," having been prepared to step into the role of Army for the live broadcast at the last minute if the comedian was deemed incapable of performing the task.

Maish shows up and wants to borrow what's left of Mountain's purse money from earlier that night. After everyone's gotten their cut, Mountain

CHRISTOPHER BENEDICT

more than willingly hands over the remaining $58. But Maish is in hock for $3,000 because Mountain's unforeseen expenses have been coming out of his own pocket, or so he serves up as a cheap excuse.

Mountain, meanwhile, is grappling with suddenly finding himself "on the outside looking in," trying to come to terms with the reality that his fighting days are over and that he has no rightful place alongside Maish and Army, but knowing that he also must resist becoming one of the walking dead who haunt the bar's "graveyard."

As soon as Mountain leaves to go for a walk and clear his head, Army guesses immediately why Maish needs the money so badly and how exactly he lost it. The crooked manager confirms his supposition. If it isn't abhorrent enough that Maish bet against Mountain, he admits that he found it inconceivable that he would last three rounds with 18-0 Jack Gibbons.

Mr. Henson's goon turns up again, this time giving Maish two weeks to come up with the money or face the consequences. Army makes it very clear that his allegiance lies with Mountain, asking Maish why he stays involved with this sport if it has corrupted him so absolutely. Maish retorts with venomous disdain, implying that the "sport" Army is referring to is so irredeemably dirty that boxing matches ought to be held in sewers.

The following day, Army accompanies Mountain to an employment office, where a pretty and empathetic social worker named Grace Carney (possibly a subtle homage to Serling favorite Art Carney) tries earnestly to find a respectable vocation for this needful ninth grade dropout from Kennesaw, Tennessee seated before her. Once the fifth-ranked heavyweight in the whole world when Joe Louis, Ezzard Charles and Jersey Joe Walcott still prowled around the top of the division, the 33-year-old prizefighter of fourteen years who never took a dive in 111 bouts is open to working any job which will help ease Maish's financial woes, whereas his manager's motives are purely self-involved.

Grace's good intentions result in an embarrassing gaffe when she attempts to reassure Mountain by explaining that she had previously worked with disfigured veterans of the war who had "special problems." About to exit her office, Mountain turns back and proudly declares that he may be a "big ugly slob" and "look like a freak" but was "almost the heavyweight champion of the world." He slams both fists down on Grace's desk for emphasis and hurts his hand. He assuages Grace's concern by confessing that pain is something he's gotten used to. Now, he says, it's "like an old friend." Grace promises to find Mountain something he will like and looks utterly devastated when she watches him walk away.

The part of Grace Carney is played by the lovely and very talented Kim Hunter, who made her screen debut in *The Seventh Victim*, a 1943 thriller from RKO producer Val Lewton. She is best remembered as Stella to Marlon Brando's Stanley Kowalski in the stage and screen versions of *A Streetcar Named Desire*, as well as Zira to Roddy McDowall's Cornelius in two of the first three *Planet of the Apes* films. Being unavailable for *Beneath* due to a scheduling conflict, McDowall was temporarily replaced by David Watson.

Hunter's career briefly hit the skids when hers was one of the names named by *Streetcar* director Elia Kazan during his notorious 1952 testimony before the House Un-American Activities Committee. Thanks to offers for consistent television work, however, she was able to rebound. A handful of the opportunities she received were teleplays written by Rod Serling, the first of which was 1955's "Portrait in Celluloid" for the *Climax!* series, followed by "Requiem," the Emmy-winning "The Comedian" costarring Mickey Rooney, and "The Dark Side of the Earth," all for *Playhouse 90*.

Hunter spoke reverently about the "beautifully put together" scripts of Serling's she had the good fortune to be attached to and recalled the time she got to reconnect with him during the shooting of *Planet of the Apes*, when Rod stopped by the courtroom set for a visit. Though it was written by Jack Laird and not Serling, Hunter appeared in a short *Night Gallery* segment called "The Late Mr. Peddington" during the series' second season.

Serling had misgivings about the way the caring social worker came across in "Requiem." With that said, Serling was quick to point out that the fault did not lie with Kim Hunter and instead admitted that the part "probably could have been better drawn." Hunter concurred with what has often been discussed as one of Serling's shortcomings as a writer, which was scripting one- dimensional female characters. Having discussed this dilemma with him, she said Rod owned up to it and put his trust in the women to flesh out the roles he wrote for them.

Back at the hotel, Maish comes clean to Army about his plan to partner with the wrestling promoter, Mr. Pirelli, and have Mountain make the rounds of the grunt and grapple circuit. He would become Harland McClintock "The Mountaineer," with a suitably ridiculous outfit to compliment his gimmick. While Maish paces around the room giving a self-aggrandizing speech about how a full stomach is worth sacrificing one's pride, all Army can say as he repeatedly shuffles a deck of cards is, "Hey Maish, you stink."

Mountain is so engrossed in 'Slapsie' Maxie's lively reverie that he hasn't even noticed Grace standing right beside him at the bar until everyone else does, and the ghosts in the "graveyard" suddenly and eerily go silent at the trespassing of a woman upon their domain. She asks Mountain whether he would consider working with children. Rod Serling himself had an opportunity to help youths when he served as a counselor at a swimming camp for kids while attending Antioch College with an eye toward a future in physical education. He also interned for a time as an attendant at a hospital for rheumatic children.

Grace counteracts Mountain's reluctance with some tough but well-meaning affirmation then catches him off guard by asking if they can have a beer together and listen to some music on the jukebox. Completely but delightfully disarmed, Mountain confesses that the only song he is familiar with is the "National Anthem" because they play it before every main event. There was, however, one boxer he remembers fondly named Smiley Collins who could "knock down a wall with his right hand" but also paradoxically played the violin.

Grace is enjoying Mountain's company, but she is sad that every topic of conversation, including a childhood trip down memory lane regarding his father, inevitably circles back around to boxing. "There isn't much else is there? Besides fighting?" she wonders aloud to Mountain. She knows there is so much more that life has to offer this tragic, resilient man with cauliflower ears and a kind heart, even if his undying trust in Maish is clearly misplaced and not returned in kind. Mountain hails Grace a cab, and their parting is a heart-tugging goodbye scene, with director Ralph Nelson allowing the shot to linger on the contemplative, lovestruck boxer watching the taxi pull away.

Maish, Army, and Mr. Pirelli are awaiting Mountain's arrival back at the hotel, and Mr. Henson places a call to Maish as a not-so-friendly reminder to make good on his past-due payment. All Mountain wants to do is discuss his date with Miss Carney, but Pirelli is eager to get down to business. Trying to make Mountain get a grasp on the workings of the wrestling racket is a difficult proposition, not least of all because his pride will not allow him to lay down for an opponent in accordance with pro wrestling's pre-determined "one night you win, the next night the other guy wins" ethos.

The way Maish sees it, however, Mountain's participation in the following evening's wrestling card is a foregone conclusion. Maish reprimands the browbeaten boxer, yelling that he owes him after everything he's done for Mountain. In an incredibly moving performance by Ed Wynn, Army lectures Maish, telling him that he'll "rot in the gutter" for essentially selling Mountain's flesh on the open market. Army accepts Maish's offer to be in Mountain's corner for the wrestling match, if only to ensure that the man he genuinely cares for is not made to play the fool. Even so, Army cannot comprehend why "so many people have to feed off one guy's misery."

Having promised to give Maish an advance on his salary for Mountain's wrestling debut, Pirelli is conferring with a pair of grapplers in the dressing room who are working out the choreographed sequence of maneuvers for their bout. Ted Christy and Ivan Rasputin not only played professional wrestlers on TV, but both had also been performing in the squared circle since the 1930s.

Born Hyman Max Fishman to Ukrainian Jews who had fled Eastern Europe and settled in Chelsea, Massachusetts, Rasputin first employed ring monikers like Hymie Fishman and Max Fishman which incorporated his given name. He later decided to merge the despotic first tsar of Russia with the Siberian mystic who played a sinister role in the termination of the Romanov dynasty into one fiendish personality for the creation of his character, Ivan 'The Terrible' Rasputin.

He was well ahead of the curve in skillfully drawing heat with fans by way of portraying a Russian villain the way Ivan and Nikita Koloff, Boris Zhukov, and Nikolai Volkoff would exploit America's xenophobic fears during the Cold War. Even my uncle, Felix Szczygiel (of Polish lineage), got in on the act by assuming the identity of Boris Sinkoff 'The Russian Cosmonaut' during his short-lived professional wrestling career on the Long Island independent circuit in the 1970s.

A two-time Pacific Coast heavyweight champion, Ivan Rasputin competed for the world title on three occasions, all losses. His first shot came opposite Bruno Nagurski in 1938 when there was only one unified world champion, followed by two cracks at the prestigious NWA (National Wrestling Alliance) title, against Orville Brown and the legendary Lou Thesz. He has only two other acting credits to his name: 1949's *Mighty Joe Young*, in which he had a bit part as a strongman, and the Gary Cooper film *Friendly Persuasion* (released a month and a half after "Requiem" aired), where Rasputin again took on the role of a wrestler, this one named Billy Goat.

Ted Christy's journey through the world of professional wrestling would span four decades by the time all was said and done in 1967. A journeyman who lost more matches than he won, Christy would claim his only title belt while working a five-month stint in Hawaii between November 1961 and

April 1962. There, he twice sharing their regional version of the NWA tag team championship with his partner, Shoulders Newman.

Over the course of his career, Christy had the opportunity to work high-profile bouts against some of the more recognizable names in the wrestling business of that era, going toe to toe with the likes of Gene LeBell, Bobo Brazil, Fritz von Erich, Stu Hart, Larry Hennig, Nick Bockwinkel, Ernie Ladd, Giant Baba, Edouard Carpentier, and even former heavyweight boxing champion Primo Carnera. In *The Twilight Zone* episode "What's in the Box," Christy played the part of The Wild Panther who was engaged in fisticuffs with The Russian Duke in the wrestling match that William Demarest's character, Joe Britt, is watching on television.

Aside from their staged tussle in "Requiem for a Heavyweight," Ted Christy and Ivan Rasputin squared off against one another at least three times in the ring. After wrestling to a draw in St. Louis in March 1951, they returned to the Gateway to the West two weeks later to stand in opposite corners for a six-man tag team match in which Christy's squad emerged victorious. Following a two-year absence from one another, the two would resume hostilities in Los Angeles, with Rasputin defeating Christy in a singles bout. Coincidentally, Ted Christy and Ivan Rasputin died exactly two weeks apart from each other in September 1976.

As for Harlan McClintock 'The Mountaineer,' he instantly regrets that he looks like "a clown" in his ring gear and is read the riot act by Maish, who inadvertently blurts out that he lost his money betting against Mountain. Turning on Maish, Mountain calls him a "dirty, lousy fink." The notion of having to enter a boxing ring "barehanded against a guy with a cleaver" wouldn't hurt as much, he insists, as the shame of going through with this charade. When Army tries to apologize to Mountain for his role in the duplicity, the boxer, in a blind rage, turns and slugs his loyal trainer. Figuring he had it coming, Army consoles a conscience-stricken Mountain.

Army meets with Grace outside the hotel bar, handing her a one-way ticket to Kennesaw, Tennessee for her to pass on to Mountain, who is inside, lurking uncertainly around the perimeter of specters telling ghost stories in "the graveyard." While she isn't necessarily sure that she loves him, she confesses to Army that she feels so sorry for him she could cry.

Grace gives Mountain the train ticket and a kiss on the cheek, assuring him that, while home may or may not be in Kennesaw, "wherever it is, it's not over there," motioning toward "the graveyard." Mountain sheepishly returns her kiss on the cheek and thanks Grace for not running away.

A young boy on the train, played by Charles Herbert (who would later appear on *The Twilight Zone* as little Tom Rogers with the robotic grandmother in Ray Bradbury's "I Sing the Body Electric,") identifies Mountain as a prizefighter by his cauliflower ears. Initially uncomfortable with the attention, Mountain quickly warms to the boy. "Requiem" comes to a close with the two beginning to bond as Mountain teaches the youngster how to maintain proper form while throwing a punch.

The Twilight Zone would often take into consideration how one of its denizens treated children—and, conversely, how innocent and impressionable little ones responded to them—as a sort of moral measuring stick by which their value as human beings was assessed. Examples include Ed Wynn's portrayal as pitchman Lew Bookman in "One for the Angels," Orson Bean as the zither-music-loving oddball "Mr. Bevis," Carol Burnett's klutzy movie theater usherette Agnes Grep in "Cavender is Coming," and a good-hearted but skeptical boxer named Bolie Jackson played by Ivan Dixon in "The Big, Tall Wish." By those virtuous standards of kindness to children, Mountain McClintock passes Serling's respectability test with flying colors.

***

Nervously pacing while chain smoking and guzzling coffee, Rod Serling watched the *Playhouse 90* production of "Requiem for a Heavyweight" at the Westport, Connecticut home of his friends, the Bergs. Ever his own worst critic, Serling observed that the conclusion of "Requiem" was "weak" and "anticlimactic." He felt he should have followed his gut instinct and ended it on a more ambiguous note with Mountain accepting the kindness of Grace and the two parting ways rather than the overly sentimental scene between Palance and the little boy on the train, which he felt was "unnecessary and diluting."

Overall, however, Serling was very pleased with how well his teleplay translated from page to screen and thought that it benefited immeasurably from the "creative direction and superb acting performances." Jack Palance in particular was singled out for considerable accolades by the writer, who raved about the dignity and decency the actor had bestowed onto Mountain McClintock.

Born in 1919 in the mining town of Lattimer, Pennsylvania to Ukrainian immigrants named Ivan and Anna, Palance has a birth certificate bearing the name Volodymyr Ivanovich Palahniuk. Before moving on to attend Hazle Township High School, he entered a local boxing contest at the age of fourteen and tied for first place with a boy three years his senior. He was the recipient of a football scholarship to the University of North Carolina, but he dropped out after just one year to go home and work in the coal mines like his father Ivan before him.

At some point in between leaving North Carolina and arriving back in Pennsylvania, Palahniuk evidently made a detour to Louisville, Kentucky, where he began preparing for a career in boxing under the guidance of Max Novich. A graduate of UNC, Novich was then studying for his bachelor's degree in medical sciences at the University of Louisville. He would later give boxing lessons to troops going through basic training during World War II and become a pioneer in sports medicine. He would use his position in that field to advocate for safer measures to protect prizefighters, such as the use of thumbless gloves and the ability of a certified ringside physician to stop a fight at their discretion.

Later that year, the 6-foot-3, nearly 200-pound Palahniuk returned to Hazleton and changed his name to Jack Brazzo, boxing as an amateur against local club fighters between late 1939 and April 1940. He reportedly won twelve out of thirteen bouts during that time, all by way of knockout.

Jack Brazzo's first professional fight would turn out to also be his last. On December 17, 1940, at the Westchester County Center in White Plains, New York, Brazzo came out on the short end of a four-round decision against Joe Baksi. Also hailing from Pennsylvania, (Marion Heights in his case), and having done an almost obligatory tour of duty down in the mines, Baksi was competing that night in the tenth of what would be 73 career bouts, compiling a 61-9-3 record.

Baksi won two out of three fights against top heavyweight contender Lee Savold in 1944 and later battered Freddie Mills so badly that the ill-fated Brit was forced to surrender from his stool on his home soil. However, Baksi would drop a wide decision to Jersey Joe Walcott and ask referee Ruby Goldstein to call a halt to his bout with soon-to-be heavyweight champion Ezzard Charles after eleven rounds, as he was no longer able to see out of his swollen left eye. All things considered, Baksi may be best known for ending the boxing career of the man we know and love as Jack Palance.

After getting punched in the Adam's apple, which left him unable to talk for a week afterwards, and losing a four-round decision for a measly 200 bucks, Palance decided that acting would be a more suitable - and definitely less hazardous - career path. Marlon Brando might not have shared the same perspective after a vigorous workout gone wrong with Palance one day.

An understudy in the role of Stanley Kowalski in the Broadway production of *A Streetcar Named Desire*, Palance was invited by Brando to take a few whacks at the punching bag Marlon had suspended from the ceiling of the theater's boiler room. An errant fist accidentally hit Brando in the face, breaking his nose. The show's star was sent to the hospital, and Palance stepped onto a Broadway stage for the first time that night as a result.

Thirty-five years before celebrating his Oscar win for Best Supporting Actor as Curly in *City Slickers* by doing one- armed pushups on stage at the age of 73, "Requiem for a Heavyweight" would earn Jack Palance the first formal recognition of his thespic talents courtesy of an Emmy award for Best Single Performance by an Actor.

Palance's was one of six wins for "Requiem" at the 1957 Emmys, the others being for Best Single Program, Best New Program Series for *Playhouse 90*, Best Direction, One Hour or More for Ralph Nelson, and Best Art Direction, One Hour or More for Albert Heschong.

Last but certainly not least, Rod Serling won his second Emmy for Best Teleplay Writing. He subsequently received a Peabody Award, the first ever given out by that foundation in recognition of exemplary television writing.

ROUND
6

Requiem for a Heavyweight: The Motion Picture (1962)

"This is a crazy fucking business," Joe Louis mumbled in the presence of his two-time ring rival Jersey Joe Walcott, with whom he occupied the dressing room of Washington DC's Uline Arena on the night of March 16, 1956. Walcott was there to officiate Louis' debut as a professional wrestler against 'Cowboy' Rocky Lee, a 320-pound journeyman grappler with facial features that were a composite of Lon Chaney Jr. and Charles Laughton.

A morning snowstorm changed over to a steady freezing rain, which kept the number of curiosity seekers inside the 9,000-seat arena down to less than half capacity. The weather was bad for business, and the whole scenario was bad for Louis. More than $1 million in debt to the IRS, which had unjustly taxed him on the purses for a pair of 1942 title defenses which were donated in full to the armed forces and seized the trust funds set up for his two children as collateral, he desperately needed the money. But what price dignity?

Battering his way through the color barrier placed in his path with a dynamite-packed right hand, Louis had punched his way to boxing's promised land to become the first Black heavyweight champion since Jack Johnson's historic and controversial reign had ended more than two decades prior. If his was a household name before June 22, 1938, Joe Louis' first-round knockout of the German former champion Max Schmeling in their rematch at Yankee Stadium that night made him a national hero.

And yet here he was, 41 years old, with a paunchy belly and a receding hairline, but with his glory days still visible in the rearview mirror without having to strain his eyes too hard to see, preparing to make the long, humbling walk to a wrestling ring assembled in the center of a hockey arena, where he would encounter his adversary for the evening—as well as the man in the striped shirt who had twice given Louis all he could handle, and then some, in their two heavyweight title fights. But that was then. This was now.

Joe Louis, the legendary 'Brown Bomber,' the former undisputed heavyweight champion of the world, hoisted up a pair of wrestling trunks and swallowed his pride to collect bumps, bruises, and a $1,050.00 paycheck. Louis' endeavor as a professional wrestler came to a violent and abrupt end a mere two and a half months later in Columbus, Ohio. For that matter, Louis himself almost did too.

'Cowboy' Rocky Lee, once again slated to tussle with Louis, overenthusiastically stomped on his opponent's chest and cracked three ribs, one shard coming close to tearing through Joe's cardiac muscles which could very well have punctured either his heart or lung. Despite the physical agony Louis was experiencing, he later said that his first concern at that very moment was, "Oh shit. There goes that good dollar."

***

Following the success of Serling's *Playhouse 90* broadcast, "Requiem for a Heavyweight" had been adapted by the BBC the following year for a televised production starring a pre-Bond Sean Connery and featuring Michael Caine in a bit part. Dutch television put on its own version in 1959, and "Requiem" would subsequently be produced in Yugoslavia in 1974.

Serling originally wanted to breathe new life into "Requiem for a Heavyweight" not on nationwide movie screens but on a single stage beneath the bright lights of Broadway. He would remain somewhat dejected because he was unable to see this dream come to fruition in his lifetime. For what it's worth, the 1985 staging of "Requiem" at New York's Martin Beck Theatre was an unmitigated disaster.

Starring John Lithgow as Mountain McClintock and featuring George Segal (Pops on *The Goldbergs*) as Maish, David Proval (*The Sopranos, Everybody Loves Raymond*) as Army, and Mari Tucci (*Law & Order*) as Grace, "Requiem" ran eight nights of previews before officially premiering on March 7, 1985. It closed just two days later, after just three performances. *New York Magazine* theater critic John Simon pulled no punches in his review of "Requiem," which he ridiculed as "melodramatic claptrap" and "morally confused."

Although converting his teleplay into a feature film was not Serling's first option, movie producer David Susskind, with whom Serling had enjoyed working previously on television, envisioned this adaptation as a viable, logical next step and enthusiastically championed the project from its conception. As he had done with "Patterns" before, Serling hoped he could make lightning strike twice with "Requiem."

It is very possible he was referencing both himself and the characters he wrote about when Serling acknowledged that society's tendency to be "quick to crown and quick to reject" is part of human nature. Whether the medium in question is sports, politics, film, music, journalism, or any number of other outlets, there are myriad examples of pop culture figures hoisted onto our collective shoulders and placed on pedestals erected at messianic heights only to be dragged back down by mobs bearing metaphorical torches and crucified in a kangaroo court of public opinion.

Betrayed and driven into financial ruin by the very country he so proudly represented in the boxing ring, including nearly 100 exhibitions staged during World War II while he was a member of the U.S. Army, Joe Louis was one such tragic hero. Even if he doesn't reference Louis specifically, instead discussing in cryptic and anonymous terminology the boxers who comprised the patchwork protagonist of the film version of *Requiem*, the fact that Serling renamed him Louis 'Mountain' Rivera certainly appears to be a signpost pointing in the former heavyweight champion's direction. Serling had once praised Joe Louis as "the greatest fighter, pound-for-pound, who ever lived," which lends credence to the suggestion that the sad downfall of the 'Brown Bomber' had partially inspired this iteration of Mountain.

Anthony Quinn appeared as a strong-armed and underhanded promoter in the 1941 Warner Bros. fight film *Knockout*, the exact antithesis of his sympathetic role as Mountain Rivera. He was best known at the time *Requiem* was made for his Academy Award-winning performance in Elia Kazan's *Viva Zapata!* in support of Marlon Brando as the film's lead. Quinn also inherited the role of Quasimodo from Lon Chaney and Charles Laughton before him for a 1956 remake of *The Hunchback of Notre Dame* and portrayed Gauguin in Vincent Minnelli's *Lust for Life* that same year, for which he won the Oscar for Best Supporting Actor. He later starred in *The Salamander*, a 1983 film based on Serling's adaptation of the novel by Morris West. This was the last screenplay Serling would complete before his untimely death in 1975.

Just like Jack Palance before him, Anthony Quinn also had a short-lived career as a boxer. A fearless and free-spirited junior high school dropout who lived with his grandmother in East Los Angeles, Quinn was constantly doing his best to elude truant officers while hustling to make a buck any way he could. During the week, he would work a variety of odd jobs. These included overseeing the assembly line in a spring factory, shining shoes, buffing floors, driving a cab, and warming up racecars at the Ascot Speedway. On weekends, Tony unloaded trucks by day and entered dance contests that offered cash prizes at night.

The morning after finding out a friend of his had been doing pretty well for himself by boxing, Quinn visited a squalid little gym on Spring Street to meet with a matchmaker who booked local smokers. Giving his true weight but lying about his age, sixteen-year-old Tony was assigned a four-round welterweight fight in Gardena. Despite his assessment that he couldn't dent an aluminum can with his punches, Quinn won easily and rode a streetcar home with a $5 purse in his pocket and a head filled with fantasies of becoming a famous boxer.

Indeed, Tony's prizefighting aspirations got off to a good start. He won his next ten bouts, signed on with a credible manager named Jim Foster, trained at the famous Main Street Gym, worked out with junior-welterweight world champion Mushy Callahan and bantamweight contender Newsboy Brown, sparred with soon-to-be heavyweight champ Primo Carnera, started moving up the card from prelims to semi-windups (the fight before the main event), and was making as much as $50 per bout. Quinn's grandmother, who initially put up a great deal of resistance to his fledgling boxing career, even handcrafted a robe for him to wear to the ring.

Though he fell in love with pugilism and the spoils of war that came with it, Tony found out the hard way one night in Long Beach that he lacked the killer instinct necessary to truly cut it in the blood-in-your-eyes fight game. Under the circumstances, you can hardly blame him.

Matched opposite a Black boxer, Quinn was disgusted by the racist taunts being hurled at his opponent from the standing-room-only crowd but tried his best to keep his head in the fight for the first four competitive rounds. The spectators were thrown into a shared frenzy when Tony drove his adversary across the ring and back against the ropes with a left hook, a right to the body, and another left hook in the fifth. Obscenities rained down on the ring in an ever-increasing torrent of bigotry.

The epithets left him unwilling to further capitalize on his opponent's obviously vulnerable state, and Quinn eased up on his offensive attack rather than put him away. The tables turned in the next, and what turned out to be the last, round, where Quinn would find himself dumped onto the canvas by a right hook and listening to the referee conclude his ten count from one knee.

Lambasted by his manager in the locker room afterwards, Quinn had to admit to himself, if not to Foster, that the fighting life was not for him. Thirty years later, however, producer Sam Spiegel dropped the script for *Requiem for a Heavyweight* in his lap to keep him occupied during a two-month hiatus from the filming of *Lawrence of Arabia*. With that, Anthony Quinn found himself back in a boxing ring.

***

The movie's pre-credit sequence begins with a tracking shot that pans slowly past a series of faces belonging to barflies and ex-fighters focused intently on the boxing match being shown on television. The ghosts of pugilism past and present who rattle their chains in this version of *Requiem's* "graveyard" include the celebrated likes of Willie Pep, Barney Ross, Abe Simon, Gus Lesnevich, Johnny Indrisano, Alex Miteff, Paolo Rosi, Tami Mauriello, and Rory Calhoun (the boxer, not the "Garrity's Sons" actor). The bout they have become so absorbed in happens to be the main event being broadcast from St. Christopher's Arena between Mountain Rivera and Cassius Clay.

In a departure from the *Playhouse 90* version of "Requiem," returning director Ralph Nelson not only stages the closing moments of the fight on camera but also allows audiences to experience the action from Mountain's point of view. The camera follows Mountain as he absorbs punch after punch from Clay's speedy hands, stares into the blinding overhead lights when he is knocked off his feet, cranes his neck to the right as the row of ringside photographers capture snapshots of his defeat and then to the left towards to spot looks of grave concern from his manager Maish and cut man Army (Jackie Gleason and Mickey Rooney, respectively), and listens without the benefit of being able to react to the ten-count administered by the increasingly out-of-focus form of Arthur Mercante. Clay consoles the still-prone Mountain before bouncing off to participate in a postmortem at center ring.

Having worked strictly in television prior to that point, this was director Ralph Nelson's first foray into motion pictures. Rod Serling made an appearance on the April 2, 1962, episode of *Tell It To Groucho* and divulged that they had just recently finished shooting *Requiem*. Asked by the cigar-smoking, eyebrow-wiggling comedian if he himself had directed it, Serling laughed and retorted that he couldn't even direct traffic.

David Susskind had thought it only natural to personally seek out real-life ref Arthur Mercante for the part of the third man in the ring in *Requiem*. But Mercante was also called upon to fill an integral role behind the camera as technical advisor. In addition to choreographing the fight scene, Mercante was tasked with finding an honest to goodness heavyweight prospect to pummel the past-his-prime Mountain Rivera.

The very first call Mercante placed was to Bill Faversham, the main investor in a Louisville consortium which sponsored the 1960 Olympic gold medalist turned professional prizefighter, Cassius Clay. The twenty-year-old 'Louisville Lip' was eager to play the part and would not long after shun his "slave name" in favor of Muhammad Ali (meaning "The Exalted One" in Arabic) and walk the earth as another one of those persecuted gods among men alluded to earlier.

CHRISTOPHER BENEDICT

Clay couldn't help himself from clowning around on set, a more than welcome diversion to alleviate the quickly developing tension between Jackie Gleason, the hard-drinking "spontaneous genius," and Anthony Quinn, the method-acting matinee idol.

Gleason criticized every decision Quinn made regarding his characterization of Mountain for the supposedly unfavorable effects that they had on the rest of the production, up to and including Gleason's own performance. Quinn admitted that he "pushed Gleason's buttons at every turn" as a form of retaliation, and their clashes often necessitated the intervention of David Susskind. While Quinn was less than pleased by both the peacekeeping efforts and directorial style of Ralph Nelson, he found an ally in Susskind as well as Mickey Rooney, who encountered his own issues dealing with the hot-headed Gleason.

Arthur Mercante remembered Anthony Quinn as a "large, rawboned man who loved boxing." The pair would go out for lunch together during breaks in production, with Quinn still in the realistic and gruesome make-up applied by Dick Smith, an industry great soon to be held in high regard for his work on the first two *Godfather* films, *Taxi Driver*, *Altered States*, and, most memorably, *The Exorcist*.

While the crew was occupied with camera setups, Jackie Gleason would spend his downtime resting in a director's chair that had his nickname, THE GREAT ONE, emblazoned across the back. Cassius Clay liked having fun with Gleason by sitting in his chair and insisting that it was clearly meant for him since, after all, he was 'The Greatest.' He would then playfully challenge Gleason to prove otherwise, recalled Mercante. The real-life referee would later oversee two of Muhammad Ali's title fights: his first classic dustup with Smokin' Joe Frazier, and the rubber match in his trilogy against Ken Norton.

Mercante kidded Gleason that he might not want to push his luck, as he already had a losing record against heavyweight boxers. He was referring to an incident that had taken place in the late 30s, when Gleason was working in The Miami Club— a seedy nightspot in Newark, New Jersey's red-light district known as 'The Bucket of Blood.' There, he challenged the "little, fat, bald-headed" heckler sitting up front to a fight. They stepped out onto Clinton Avenue, and the next thing Gleason remembered was waking up on the floor of the club's furnace room being tended to by a doctor after getting knocked out cold by 'Two-Ton' Tony Galento.

For the uninitiated, Galento was a saloon owner and heavyweight contender from Orange, New Jersey with the type of thirst only a beer barrel could slake and a physique to match. He was what Ralph Kramden would undoubtedly refer to as a "blabbermouth," famous for growling his pre-fight prediction, "I'll moida da bum." Ironically, Galento would himself be initiated into Joe Louis' "Bum of the Month Club" in 1939, courtesy of a fourth-round knockout, but only after shocking spectators by sending Louis to the canvas in the third. He can be seen in *On the Waterfront* as one of mob-affiliated labor leader Johnny Friendly's stooges.

Former prizefighter Abie Bain plays the police officer who escorts Mountain, Maish, and Army from the ring to the dressing room. He was also an advisor to, and stand-in for, Anthony Quinn, who used Bain as a template for Mountain's speech patterns and mannerisms. The two had been in the boxing movie *Knockout* together twenty years earlier.

Born in St. Petersburg, Russia, but fighting as a middleweight out of Newark, New Jersey, Abie's career got underway in March 1923, competing in ten bouts in nine months and more or less keeping the pedal pressed to the floor the rest of the way. After gradually climbing up the scales to light-heavyweight by 1930, Abie challenged world champion 'Slapsie' Maxie Rosenbloom (who, if you recall, was featured in the *Playhouse 90* version of "Requiem") but was knocked out in the eleventh round. The following year, Bain tangled with Jackie Gleason's soon-to-be-nemesis Tony Galento and wound up flat on his back just like the roly-poly funny man would. Abie racked up nearly 200 TV and movie roles, among them playing a crew member in "The Man in the Funny Suit" (depicting the behind the scenes drama of "Requiem for a Heavyweight"), two *Playhouse 90* episodes scripted by Serling—"A Town Has Turned to Dust" and "In the Presence of Mine Enemies"—and as a reporter in Rod's political thriller *Seven Days in May*.

In name recognition if nothing else, Jackie Gleason and Mickey Rooney as Maish and Army were considered a trade-up from Keenan and Ed Wynn. In terms of performance, viewers can decide for themselves. Despite the initial misgivings regarding his casting, Ed Wynn did earn an Emmy nomination. Serling would not only employ Wynn on two occasions for *The Twilight Zone* but also write a eulogy for him, which was delivered by Jack Palance at the comedian's memorial service.

Rooney was an already familiar face to Serling, having starred in his Emmy-winning production of "The Comedian" for *Playhouse 90*. The two would become reacquainted in the fifth dimension when Mickey was cast in *The Twilight Zone* episode "Last Night of a Jockey." Rooney would addi-

CHRISTOPHER BENEDICT

tionally appear in the "Rare Objects" segment of Rod Serling's *Night Gallery*.

Mickey had played the titular character in the 1947 movie *Killer McCoy*, a bad-luck boxer who inadvertently kills an opponent and gets mixed up with the mob. Later in life, Rooney had an agent named Bob Case who also happened to be an advisor and drug rehab sponsor to Johnny Tapia, a pugilistic wild child from Albuquerque.

Consistent with his ring moniker, Mi Vida Loca (My Crazy Life), Tapia was a prizefighter with a tortured soul, a heart of gold, and a terrible cocaine addiction. He understood that he was not long for this world and lived his crazy life full throttle with this premise always lodged in his mind. Case introduced Johnny to Mickey, with whom he forged a strong and lasting connection.

Rooney was a frequent visitor to Tapia's dressing room, where he would pray with Johnny before his fights and offer words of encouragement to the three-division world champion. Tapia would win five world titles and survive an equal amount of drug overdoses. Though Johnny's heart was undeniably resilient inside the roped-off square, it had had enough of his reckless lifestyle and gave out on him one fateful afternoon at his home at the age of forty-five.

Two other noteworthy *Twilight Zone* alums turn up in *Requiem*: Herbie Faye, who plays the role of Charlie the bartender and would serve drinks again in "A Kind of Stopwatch," and Val Avery, the promoter of the young fighter presented for Maish's managerial consideration who played—you guessed it—a bartender in classic Christmas episode "Night of the Meek."

In the *Playhouse 90* version, Keenan Wynn's Maish owes money to, and is threatened by an associate of, a Mr. Henson, an enigmatic mob boss who is never pictured on camera during the program's entire run time. Serling doesn't simply rectify this matter for the movie. Serling flips the script by transforming the character into a female gangster named Ma Greeny, who very much makes her presence known. Ma Greeny is played by Bertha Levine, better known by her stage name Madame Spivy.

A former lounge singer, she would later open her own New York City nightclub called Spivy's Roof in the 1940s before turning her attention to acting. She made her debut on an episode of *Alfred Hitchcock Presents* and soon after landed the role of saloon owner Ruby Lightfoot in *The Fugitive Kind*, directed by Sidney Lumet, written by Tennessee Williams, and starring Marlon Brando. A woman who was short and rotund in stature and had no problem assuming a gruff demeanor when the situation called for it, Spivy had played a bouncer in *All Fall Down* just prior to her role as the heavy in *Requiem*. She would subsequently materialize in Frank Sinatra's dream sequence in *The Manchurian Candidate*.

Very early into the movie, an elaborate chase scene ensues where Gleason's Maish is pursued throughout the Olympic Auditorium (doubling for St. Christopher's Arena) by Ma Greeny's thugs. Her main man is played by Michael Conrad, a future visitor to *The Twilight Zone* in the form of Sheriff Harper for Season Five's "Black Leather Jackets." Ultimately, Maish finds himself trapped in the center of the ring, where he is worked over by Ma Greeny's hoodlums as incentive to speed up their cash transaction.

A pair of 1949 boxing movies both feature very similar sequences to the one described above. *The Set-Up* sees Robert Ryan's Stoker Thompson double-crossed when his manager alerts him mid-fight that he needs to take a dive. Stoker ignores that directive and wins the bout. He manages to outrun the goons employed by a mobster called Little Boy through the catacombs of the fictional Paradise City Arena, but has his hand broken out in the alleyway, ending his boxing career.

Similarly, Midge Kelly, played by Kirk Douglas in *Champion*, reluctantly consents to a mob-ordered fix in which he will throw a fight against number one contender Johnny Dunne with the payoff being a title shot for himself in the near future. He instead demolishes Dunne in the opening round. This noncompliance earns Kelly a thumping in the middle of the ring, much the same as happens off-camera to Maish in *Requiem*.

Starring Fred Williamson in the title role, an ultra-violent chase scene ensues near the end of the 1972 Blaxploitation boxing flick *Hammer*. Like *Requiem*, it, too, was filmed partially on location at the Olympic Auditorium. Williamson's Hammer fares much better than Maish and dispatches his would-be attackers in over-the-top fashion in the Olympic Auditorium parking garage.

With Army tagging along for moral support, Mountain answers a want ad for a job as a movie theater usher but is turned away after being rudely notified that they don't have uniforms in his size. Mickey Rooney is given the perfect opportunity to exit the scene by delivering a great one-liner, which Rod Serling no doubt crafted with deliberate pleasure: "I like TV better anyway."

This rejection brings Mountain to the employment agency where he encounters his caseworker and love interest Grace, whose last name is changed to Miller and is played this time by Julie Harris. Harris was among the first members of New York's famed Actors Studio and made her mark in Hollywood relatively early thanks to her terrific performances in two adaptations of classic novels, Carson McCullers' *The Member of the Wedding* and John Steinbeck's *East of Eden*. Shortly after *Requiem* came *The Haunting*, based on Shirley Jackson's hair-raising book. Harris was later offered a role as a series regular on *Knots Landing*, my mom's favorite nighttime soap opera and my first introduction to her.

If you happen to be a fan of *Planet of the Apes* (for which Rod Serling turned in several drafts of the initial screenplay and is credited as co-writer on the release print), this curious little bit of trivia might be of tangential interest. In *Requiem for a Heavyweight*, Julie Harris plays the role originated in the *Playhouse 90* broadcast by Kim Hunter six years earlier. Hunter, of course, was later cast as Dr. Zira in 1968's *Planet of the Apes*, a part she would play in the first three entries of the classic sci-fi film series. She came on board somewhat late in the process, however, as a replacement for the actress who was initially slated to appear in the movie—Julie Harris.

The card game that Army and Maish play back at the hotel is memorable for the way in which Jackie Gleason reacts, albeit in much more subtle tones, to Mickey Rooney's idiosyncrasies, calling to mind how Ralph Kramden would get so easily bent out of shape by his quirky pal Ed Norton on *The Honeymooners*. This wasn't just for the benefit of the cameras, however. Anthony Quinn recalled the already irritable Gleason being legitimately annoyed during the filming of this scene.

Stanley Adams returns as wrestling promoter, Perelli (slightly different spelling in this version) the lone holdover from the original cast of "Requiem." He devises an Indian chief gimmick for Mountain in this iteration, scheming with Maish toward a Cowboy vs. Indian angle for the boxer's grunt and grapple debut.

Grace, meanwhile, has set up a meeting for Mountain with a couple by the name of Reardon, who run a summer camp for kids in the Adirondacks, so that he can interview for a position as a counselor. Maish sabotages this opportunity by getting Mountain drunk, their binge starting at the hotel and winding up three sheets to the wind at Jack Dempsey's Broadway Bar, where they are seated with the ex-heavyweight champ himself before he is called away to play host to a birthday party at an adjacent table.

By the time Mountain gets to the Hotel St. Moritz, he is in no condition to make a good impression on his potential employers. He forgets their room number and staggers up and down the tenth-floor hallway yelling the Reardons' name and banging on random doors. He carelessly upsets a room service cart, and the clamor brings Grace out of the Reardons' room. Before she can intervene and possibly salvage the situation, a rueful Mountain retreats to the elevator.

Grace follows Mountain back to his shabby hotel room, where he reminds her that his scars aren't medals and that the reason he talks so funny is because he's "been hit a million times." Even though getting plastered and lousing up the interview was Maish's idea, Mountain admits that he was knowingly complicit in undermining the chance to prove his self-worth. A tender scene becomes momentarily fraught with savagery as Mountain pulls Grace down onto his bed and begins to force himself on her. He quickly backs off, however, and apologetically tells her to go, conceding sadly that "I belong with dirty towels in locker rooms."

On her way out of the hotel, Grace runs into Maish on the stairwell. With a sense of smug self-satisfaction, he tells her to go find another charity case then makes matters even worse by comparing Mountain to a trained ape wearing clothes. Grace slaps him across the face and turns away crying. Devoid of empathy, Maish advises her to leave Mountain alone so that he can keep chasing ghosts like he has been for most of his adult life.

The hotel's desk clerk who informs Maish that Mountain is upstairs with Miss Miller was played by middleweight contender Steve Belloise. Coming up just a little short in two consecutive 1940 title shots against Ken Overlin at Madison Square Garden, Belloise subsequently scored a first-round knockout of his *Requiem* costar Tami Mauriello. He also dispatched both Al Hostak and Georgie Abrams well inside the distance, although he would lose his rematch with Hostak on points. He was unable to answer the bell for the eighth round in a 1949 world middleweight title eliminator against Sugar Ray Robinson at Yankee Stadium and was stopped in his last two bouts by Laurent Dauthuille and Billy Kilgore. His final ring record was a more than respectable 95-13-3 with 59 KOs. Ring 10, a non-profit organization based out of Long Island which provides financial assistance to former fighters in need, named their Top Contender of the Year Award after the Bronx-born Belloise, who passed away in 1984.

The most radical divergence Serling makes from the televised broadcast of "Requiem for a Heavyweight" to the feature film can be seen in the tonal discord between the two productions' unique endings. After standing up for himself, Jack Palance's Mountain McClintock is bestowed a happy ending where he teaches a young boy how to box aboard a train heading home to Kennesaw, Tennessee, where he will work as a camp counselor. In the motion picture, however, Anthony Quinn's Mountain Rivera remains shackled to his devotion to Maish and is summarily doomed to a bleak, pessimistic fate.

With a four-way midget free-for-all in progress inside the ring, Mountain puts up an admirable fight against Ma Greeny's henchmen in the dressing room but ultimately agrees to an eight-match contract with Perelli, with an option for sixteen more, rather than have Maish take a severe beating or even worse for non-payment of his debt.

Outfitted in a braided hairpiece and headdress and enveloped in a Navajo blanket, Mountain makes his way to the ring amidst a chorus of boos, jeers, and oaths past the midget wrestlers, one of whom is played by Angelo Rossitto. Standing just under three feet tall, Rossitto had a lengthy acting career which dated back to the silent era in the late 20s. His most significant, and sometimes notorious, screen appearances came in Tod Browning's *Freaks* (in which he dances across the table at the wedding feast of Hans and Cleopatra, passing around the communal loving cup only to have Olga Baclanova throw its contents in his face), *March of the Wooden Soldiers*, *The Wizard of Oz*, Poverty Row quickies like *The Corpse Vanishes* and *Scared to Death* with Bela Lugosi, *Confessions of an Opium Eater* featuring Vincent Price, *Dracula vs. Frankenstein*, and *Mad Max Beyond Thunderdome*.

Matched against real-life wrestling behemoth Haystacks Calhoun, who reportedly tipped the scales at 600-plus pounds and wore overalls as his ring attire, with a horseshoe on a chain around his neck, "Big Chief Mountain" stares around the arena with a blank, almost disbelieving expression for a few moments before raising a tomahawk above his head, belting out a series of war cries, and dancing in circles while the introductions are made and Army watches from the wings and weeps.

***

Given a mostly lukewarm reception by both critics and moviegoers, *Requiem* failed to pack much of a punch at the box office. With a reported budget of $1.1 million, the film scarcely turned a profit after pulling in a modest domestic gross (U.S. and Canada) of $1.3 million, putting it in thirty- seventh place 1962, behind far more heavy-hitting releases like *The Longest Day*, *Lawrence of Arabia* (also featuring Anthony Quinn), *To Kill a Mockingbird, Lolita, The Manchurian Candidate* (also featuring Madame Spivy), *The Man Who Shot Liberty Valance, Cape Fear,* and *Whatever Happened to Baby Jane?*

To add insult to injury, the movie failed to match the acclaim of its much-heralded small screen predecessor during the awards season. Aside from being named one of the National Board of Review's Top Ten Films of the year, the movie version of *Requiem* fell victim to a technical knockout.

No validation whatsoever for the labors of cast or crew was forthcoming from the Academy of Motion Picture Arts and Sciences. Ralph Nelson was in the running for a Director's Guild statuette, but lost out to David Lean, and Mickey Rooney was considered for a Golden Laurel for Top Male Supporting Performance with that prize going to Gig Young, who had starred three years earlier in Serling's autobiographical *Twilight Zone* classic "Walking Distance."

Disappointing as it must have been for those involved, *Requiem for a Heavyweight* cannot be measured solely by lackluster cash receipts and award nominations. For all its real or perceived shortcomings, the film still accomplished what it set out to do. Regardless of whether most agree that *Requiem* qualifies as such, great art, it has been said, is intended to comfort the disturbed and disturb the comfortable.

Anthony Quinn was proud of the fact that *Requiem* didn't take half-measures in forcing the audience to feel like active participants in creating the conditions that precipitated the crumbling of Mountain Rivera. He even went so far as to refer to the movie as a kind of "protest."

Quinn's frank assessment goes hand in hand with that of the film's writer. First cautioning that tragedy should not be mistaken for misery, Rod Serling stated in no uncertain terms that he crafted with deliberate forethought a lamentable tale that was "honest" and "uncompromising."

That said, Serling is certainly in the minority with his personal opinion of *Requiem* as "not a very good picture." Generally, he felt the film was "badly directed" and "poorly performed" aside from Jackie Gleason and Mickey Rooney. It's safe to say that most modern-day fight fans and film buffs would respectfully disagree.

ROUND
7

Trying to Catch That Bus to Glory in The Twilight Zone

The Big, Tall Wish

In the approximate mold of Danny Fales, Scotty Beckitt, Steve Garrity, and Mountain McClintock before him, Bolie Jackson is a past-his-prime prizefighter with a fatalistic mindset who, as he tells it, is "running down the street trying to catch that bus to glory." Rod Serling's latest pugilistic also-ran reached televisions tuned to CBS on the evening of April 8, 1960, through "The Big, Tall Wish," the twenty-seventh episode of the first season of *The Twilight Zone.*

Serling's fallen heroes of the boxing world often mourn the passing of championship opportunities that have come and gone or pine away for chances that never present themselves. Bolie Jackson, aside from his skin color (which necessitates further discussion momentarily), has one major factor that distinguishes him from the rest.

Bolie's lifeline, his primary source of support and encouragement, is not a caring social worker, kind-hearted trainer, or estranged brother who has found his way to forgiveness. It is Henry Temple, a nine-year-old boy who has been endowed by The Twilight Zone with the ability to make his wishes—the titular big, tall wish, specifically—come true. When and how he chooses to use this gift reveals everything about little Henry and his "good and close friend" Bolie. And, for that matter, Rod Serling himself.

Rod's daughter Anne Serling writes in her memoir, *As I Knew Him: My Dad, Rod Serling*, about first seeing "The Big, Tall Wish" years after her father had died. She feels that the episode's sentimentality in no way detracts from its "edge of steel" and "never glosses over the harsh reality of day-to-day survival for the poor and marginalized."

***

Rod Serling proclaimed during a speech given at the Library of Congress in 1968 that "the writer's role is to menace the public's conscience." Serling developed *The Twilight Zone* with that same spirit after repeated run-ins with television executives and interference from network sponsors over the topical content of certain teleplays. The best example of this was Serling's attempts to dramatize the murder of Emmett Till, which made already skittish decision makers especially uneasy.

A science fiction anthology program was the perfect Trojan horse, a vehicle enabling Serling to fill viewer's living rooms with far-out tales that were purely for entertainment on a superficial level but contained contemporary allegories hidden within. The moral of the story could be delivered with a heavy hand on some occasions, as Serling did like a punch to the solar plexus with episodes such as "The Monsters Are Due on Maple Street," "The Shelter," "Deaths-Head Revisited," "I Am the Night, Color Me Black," "The Gift," and "He's Alive."

All things considered, Serling had come to the conclusion that "it was alright to have Martians saying things Democrats and Republicans could never say." Commenting on how significantly he was forced to compromise his script for what was supposed to have been a hard-hitting political drama called "The Arena" for *Studio One* in 1956, Serling grumbled that he should have set it in the year 2057 and populated the Senate with robots.

Obviously, *The Twilight Zone* was so much more than just Martians and robots. The cautionary tales composed by Serling (who wrote 92 of the 156 episodes), Richard Matheson, Charles Beaumont, George Clayton Johnson, Earl Hamner Jr. and other talented writers throughout the course of the show's five seasons dealt with a variety of genres inhabited by creatures of unnatural or extraterrestrial origin as well as carbon-based human beings from all walks of life, including prizefighters. Of course, one of *The Twilight Zone's* boxers happened to be a mechanized automaton, but we'll get to that a little later. Right now, though, let's get back to Bolie Jackson.

***

Bolie tells his faithful little admirer Henry that a fighter's flesh is like a scrapbook. Lost in self-reflection, Bolie verbally catalogs the inventory of painful physical reminders collected throughout his career: the ridged flesh above his right brow from a fight with Sailor Levitt in St. Louis in 1949; the crooked bridge of his flattened nose which was broken twice in the same bout at Syracuse's Memorial Stadium by an Italian boy who fought like Henry Armstrong; a scar running the length of his right cheek from being raked by the laces of an opponent's glove one night in Miami. All told, Bolie's facial features comprise a topographical road map to the wasteland of discarded dreams.

Radio and television historian Martin Grams Jr. suggests in his comprehensive volume *The Twilight Zone Unlocking the Door to a Television Classic* that Archie Moore was first cast in the role of Bolie Jackson but was replaced by Ivan Dixon. There is no mention of this in any of the books by or about 'The Old Mongoose,' but "The Big, Tall Wish" was rehearsed and filmed on the MGM lot between February 19 and 26, 1960. This time frame coincides with Archie's extended stay in Los Angeles to appear in *The Ad-*

ventures of Huckleberry Finn, playing the part of runaway slave and Huck's travel companion Jim from Mark Twain's classic novel. In fact, Moore was stripped of his light-heavyweight title in 1960 due to his prolonged ring inactivity. So, Grams' claim is entirely within the realm of possibility.

Another tangential connection linking Moore to the fifth dimension is his comment supposedly about being on the receiving end of a knockdown during a title defense against Yvon Durelle: "Man, I was in The Twilight Zone." Although Martin Grams Jr. is mistaken about the date and result— he reports it as a 1961 knockout loss at Durelle's hands despite the fact that Archie was victorious in both bouts against New Brunswick's 'Fighting Fisherman' by way of KO, in 1958 and '59—I am assuming he meant Moore getting viciously cold-cocked by a right haymaker one minute into the first round of their first fight.

Durelle would floor 'The Old Mongoose' twice more in the opening stanza and once again in the fifth but would get sent to the deck four times himself, finally counted out by referee and former heavyweight champion Jack Sharkey in the eleventh round. Moore would proceed in putting Durelle away in the third round of their rematch eight months later.

Unfortunately, I couldn't trace Archie's *Twilight Zone* reference to an original source, and the show's premiere episode wouldn't air for more than a month and a half after the Moore/Durelle rematch. This appears to be one of those apocryphal, too-good-to-be-true stories we want to believe even when the evidence just isn't there.

With an intense look that belies the youthful contours of his face, Henry snaps his fingers and hops down off Bolie's dresser. He insists that the aging boxer has been hurt enough before saying that he is going to make a "big, tall wish" that will see Bolie through an upcoming fight. Henry's mother Frances informs Bolie that she too was the recipient of the "big, tall wish." Fifteen dollars behind on the rent, Frances received a check in the mail for exactly that amount as compensation for nursing services she provided to a woman from Long Island after Henry worked his magic.

Despite caring so much for Henry that he takes him to ball games and for walks in the park, Bolie feels unworthy of the child's hero worship. His own personal life experiences have hardened his resolve to the point where he is unable to reconcile a belief in anything he cannot see, feel, or be wounded by. Both boxing and the cruelty of the world at large have beaten Bolie's dreams out of him. Far removed from the wonderment of childhood, he has long since assessed hope, which is a valuable and necessary commodity for us all, to be a luxury he can no longer afford. The world Bolie lives in is made of concrete.

Making his way toward St. Nick's Arena past a small but enthusiastic congregation of well-wishers on the stoop and sidewalk in front of their apartment building, Bolie turns around to return the smile of Henry, who looks down from the ledge of his second-floor window. The young boy is secure in the knowledge that the "big, tall wish" is there for him to use if his friend needs it.

***

Now would be as good a time as any to discuss the fact that Bolie, Henry, Frances, and nearly all cast members on "The Big, Tall Wish" are African American. A production decision like this was considered unthinkable at the time and was an intentionally provocative choice on the part of Rod Serling because of his belief that Black actors were woefully underrepresented within the film and television industry. More than that, Serling viewed prejudice as humankind's greatest evil.

While "The Big, Tall Wish" did indeed honestly portray the cultural marginalization of Black Americans, Serling's representation of the racial group was a refreshing counterpoint to the harmful stereotypes so prevalent then. In fact, Serling afforded his Black characters a dignity that many of their real-life counterparts would be denied by 1960s society.

Just as Rod Serling venerated Joe Louis not just for his punching power but for his human decency, so too did the star of "The Big, Tall Wish," Ivan Dixon, who portrayed Bolie Jackson. The Harlem-born Dixon appeared in both the stage and screen versions of *A Raisin in the Sun* opposite Sidney Poitier, with whom he became and remained fast friends. Ivan served as Poitier's stunt double for *The Defiant Ones*, and the two also appeared together in *Something of Value*, *Porgy and Bess*, and *A Patch of Blue*.

After "The Big, Tall Wish," Dixon would return to *The Twilight Zone* as Reverend Anderson in "I Am the Night, Color Me Black" and receive great acclaim in the feature film *Nothing But a Man* that same year. Given Dixon's accomplishments across diverse roles, it's unfortunate that he is probably best remembered for his five-year stint on *Hogan's Heroes*, a show Rod Serling, a World War II veteran and Jewish man, detested due to its comedic depiction of a German POW camp. A president of Negro Actors for Action, Dixon was the recipient of four NAACP Image Awards, the National Black Theatre Award, and the Paul Robeson Pioneer Award from the Black American Cinema Society.

"The Big, Tall Wish" wasn't the first time that Kim Hamilton, who plays Henry's mother Frances, appeared alongside Ivan Dixon. She made her feature film debut starring alongside Dixon and Sidney Poitier with a small role in 1957's *Something of Value*, featuring Rock Hudson. Hamilton's most prominent part, even if a relatively minor one, came as Tom Robinson's wife Helen in *To Kill a Mockingbird*. She would later be cast in the 1981 remake of the boxing movie *Body and Soul*. Television would prove to be Hamilton's bread and butter, with more than five decades worth of guest spots on *Leave it to Beaver, My Three Sons, Mod Squad, All in the Family* (playing the original Helen Willis), *Sanford and Son, Good Times, The White Shadow, The Jeffersons* (not as Helen Willis), *Gimme a Break!, Star Trek: The Next Generation*, and many more besides.

Steven Perry, who plays little Henry Temple, worked with Ivan Dixon for the first time on "The Big, Tall Wish," but it would not be the last. The two would cross paths again during the filming of *A Raisin in the Sun*, when Perry won the role of Sidney Poitier's offspring, Travis. He made his acting debut at the age of six in a 1958 episode of *General Electric Theater* titled "Auf Wiedersehen," playing an orphan named, oddly enough, Joe Louis. He followed that up with *The Sound and the Fury, The Man in the Net*, and *The Rebel Breed* before his one and only visit to *The Twilight Zone*. Perry has only another dozen or so acting credits to his name, including three appearances on *Magnum P.I.* and a recurring role on *Jake and the Fatman*. He appears to have stepped away from the industry completely after the 1997 made-for-TV movie *Escape from Atlantis*.

***

Bolie is in the dressing room at St. Nick's Arena, getting his hands wrapped by his trainer Joe Mizelli (longtime character actor Walter Burke, who was later cast in the *Night Gallery* segment "Deliveries in the Rear"), when he deduces that the fight promoter by the name of Thomas (Henry Scott, who would reappear in *The Twilight Zone* for "The Thirty-Fathom Grave") has bet against him. He takes a swing at the double-crosser. Thomas manages to duck the punch and Bolie smashes his knuckles into the wall, a visual callback to his earlier comment about how easy it is to be wounded by a world made of concrete. Painfully squeezing his broken hand into a boxing glove, Bolie's lone regret seems to be how he has turned poor Henry's wish into even more of a long shot.

Director Ron Winston, who had also helmed "The Monsters Are Due on Maple Street" and would return to *The Twilight Zone* to oversee "Stopover in a Quiet Town," makes the most of a limited budget and meager cast of extras by depicting the fight audience through an effective sequence of closeup shots. We see a man pound his fist into an open palm, a woman clutch the forearm of the man seated beside her, a man wringing his hands together, a woman shielding her face with both hands, a man absent-mindedly shoveling popcorn into his mouth, a woman peeking nervously between splayed fingers, a man aggressively twisting a newspaper, a woman mimicking a fighter's defensive posture, a man picking his fingernail with a toothpick and sticking the opposite end into his mouth, and the ringside announcer gripping the microphone with both hands while describing to home viewers the terrible beating Bolie Jackson is taking at the hands of Joey Consiglio.

Charles Horvath, who portrays Consiglio in "The Big, Tall Wish," was mentioned earlier when discussing "Garrity's Sons," Serling's 1955 boxing story broadcast on *Ford Television Theatre*. The formidable-looking Horvath was famous for turning up on the silver screen and small screen alike as a cowboy, Indian, henchman, mugger, convict, bouncer, bar brawler, or prizefighter. In "Garrity's Sons," Horvath had played an over-the-hill heavyweight contender named Sammy, who sought the services of Rory Calhoun's title character. He additionally appeared as an uncredited fighter in *The Harder They Fall* and played a boxer called Champ in an episode of the TV western *Tales of the Texas Rangers*.

Henry and Frances watch the fight from home, wearing matching expressions of concern as Bolie absorbs a multitude of unanswered punches dealt out by Consiglio and crumples to the canvas. As the count of real-life ref Frankie Van approaches its inevitable conclusion, Henry presses his face to the television screen and repeats Bolie's name over and over as if chanting a magic incantation. At the count of ten, the two boxers have inconceivably traded places. Consiglio is lying on the canvas, and the referee is raising Bolie's hand.

Frankie Van, incidentally, officiated in excess of 500 professional bouts during his thirty-five-year career and appeared in more than fifty films spanning four decades, almost always as a referee in movies and TV shows like *Golden Gloves*, *Abbott and Costello Meet the Invisible Man*, *Rocky*, and Rod Serling's *Night Gallery* in "The Ring with the Red Velvet Ropes."

Upon returning home, a triumphant but bewildered Bolie recounts the bizarre events of the fight's conclusion for Henry on the roof of their tenement. Henry tries to make his friend understand that his victory was a manifestation of the "big, tall wish." To Bolie, however, magic is mumbo jumbo, and wishes are the stuff dreamt up by a "dopey kid," which he can only equate with unfulfilled promises and human misery that will break your heart. Henry understands that the magic behind his "big, tall wish" will only work if Bolie has faith in it. He tearfully implores Bolie to believe. Tragically, Bolie is too old, too skeptical, too beaten down by his life to believe in magic.

In retrospect, we see that Henry Temple and Anthony Fremont, the six-year-old freckle-faced "monster" played by Billy Mumy in the season three classic "It's a Good Life," are the antithesis of one another. They have both been granted the supernatural ability to enact great change by the Twilight Zone's powers-that-be, but each one uses his gift with very different motives in mind.

Anthony insists on the conformity of everyone around him to his way of thinking, lest they disrupt the delicate balance of order he has established within his controlled environment of manufactured happiness. Anyone who fails to think what Anthony has dictated to be good thoughts and act according to his whims will be banished to the cornfield for their transgressions. Henry, on the other hand, selflessly uses the fulfillment of his wishes to help those he loves to lead a life of quiet dignity or maybe even chase down a chance at championship glory.

The scene cuts back to the ring in St. Nick's Arena where Bolie, unable to accept what he hasn't rightfully earned and having refused Henry's wish, resumes his place on the canvas to be counted out by Frankie Van. Laying there, he watches that bus to glory he has been chasing leave the station, never to return. This time, Bolie's walk home is a solitary and solemn one. He is sporting a bandage over his left eye and a cast on his broken right hand as the latest additions to his bodily collection of boxing souvenirs.

Frances expresses her apologies and lets Bolie into Henry's room, where the little boy tells the world-weary fighter that he won't be making any more wishes because he's too old to believe in magic. Only then does Bolie take the opportunity to wistfully muse about the possibility of a world where magic might just exist.

If only more people believed, perhaps we could all live in a world where hope springs up like flowers between cracks in the concrete. That world exists in the hearts of children, and in *The Twilight Zone*.

***

Shortly after "The Big, Tall Wish" was broadcast, Rod Serling received a

CHRISTOPHER BENEDICT

letter from the National Scholarship Service and Fund for Negro Students in New York with their thanks for representing the Black community on *The Twilight Zone*. Serling replied with a letter of acknowledgement as well as a $25.00 donation to their foundation. He did likewise in response to a similar letter of gratitude from the Committee to Salvage Talent for Negro Actors, and subsequently made a donation to the NAACP in December 1960. *The Twilight Zone* was bestowed the Unity Award for Outstanding Contributions to Better Race Relations in 1961.

Two years later CBS would enact a policy to ensure more consistent hiring of Black actors.

***

As part of the anthology program *One Step Beyond*, the 1961 episode "The Last Round" features Charles Bronson playing a boxer who gets spooked by a visitation from a pugilistic specter. Those who have seen the episode may spot a nod to "The Big, Tall Wish" within it. Hanging on the wall of the promoter's office is a fight poster for the bout between Bolie Jackson and Joey Consiglio.

The Four of Us Are Dying

Strictly speaking, Bolie Jackson was not the first boxer depicted on *The Twilight Zone*. This distinction belongs to the ill-fated Andy Marshak in "The Four of Us Are Dying," which Rod Serling adapted from the short story "All of Us Are Dying" by George Clayton Johnson. While not a boxing-themed episode, it qualifies for an honorable mention nevertheless.

In his $3.80 room at the ironically named Hotel Real, 36-year-old "nickel and dime man" Arch Hammer (Harry Townes, later to appear in the Charles Beaumont-scripted "Shadow Play" and the *Night Gallery* segment "Lindemann's Catch") fans out a batch of newspaper clippings on the bedspread from which to select identities that will meet his immediate needs. Hammer possesses the ability to alter his facial features at will to resemble anyone at any time to suit any purpose.

His dangerous game of make-believe begins with putting the moves on a heartbroken lounge singer (Beverly Garland from *It Conquered the World*) hopelessly hung up on a musician named Johnny Foster (Ross Martin, who would appear in the hour-long *Twilight Zone* episode "Death Ship" as well as two *Night Gallery* segments, "Camera Obscura" and "The Other Way

Out"), who was killed when a locomotive struck his car. Since then, she has relied on bourbon and ballads to cope with her grief.

Hammer proceeds from his meeting with the lounge singer to put the squeeze on Penell, a mob boss played by Bernard Fein (a heckler in the season four episode "He's Alive," starring a young Dennis Hopper). Penell had one of his henchmen, Virgil Sterig (Phillip Pine, later to revisit *The Twilight Zone* for "The Incredible World of Horace Ford"), dumped into the river after pulling a heist to avoid paying him his rightful share of the loot. Arch came to collect that share in full.

Trapped in a dead-end alleyway by two of Penell's stooges, Hammer improvises a getaway plan by adopting the countenance of Andy Marshak, a boxer whose likeness he notices on a tattered fight poster peeling off the brick wall at his back. Marshak is portrayed by character actor Don Gordon, who would make a return trip to *The Twilight Zone* four years later to play the title role in "The Self-Improvement of Salvadore Ross."

Sure enough, Penell's thugs are fooled and thrown off the scent. Hammer, as Marshak, heads off until recognized by an elderly man running a newsstand (Peter Brocco, an uncredited space alien in "Hocus-Pocus and Frisby" and later to appear in the *Night Gallery* segment "Deliveries in the Rear"). The audience soon learns that this man is Marshak's father.

An incredulous Hammer tries to make sense of the fact that he, or rather Marshak, is this stranger's son. The old man is filled with bitter resentment over Marshak's abandonment of his own mother as well as his mistreatment of a "sweet, decent little girl." Hammer shoves Marshak's father to the ground, where the old man cries at the retreating form, "Look at the monster. Look at my son."

With his scheme gone awry, Hammer returns to the hotel, where he is collared by a detective on an outstanding bunco rap. Taking one extra spin through the hotel's revolving door, Hammer comes out on the other side as boxer Andy Marshak once again.

Just when he thinks he's pulled a fast one and is home free, the prizefighter's distraught father returns and guns him down in the street. There, Andy Marshak, Virgil Sterig, Johnny Foster, and Arch Hammer all lay dying.

CHRISTOPHER BENEDICT

Steel

Richard Matheson was one of the science fiction/horror genre's more prescient and prolific writers, inspiring future authors such as Stephen King to craft their own spine-tingling tales. It is little wonder that Rod Serling would tap into Matheson's considerable talents on sixteen occasions throughout *The Twilight Zone's* five-season run. Who can forget the classics like "Third from the Sun," "The Invaders," and the two William Shatner episodes, "Nick of Time" and "Nightmare at 20,000 Feet," that emerged from this collaboration?

Seven years before he would adapt it into a teleplay for *The Twilight Zone's* second episode of its fifth and final season, Matheson's short story "Steel" was published in the May 1956 issue of *The Magazine of Fantasy and Science Fiction*. "Steel" was an ingeniously crafted tale dealing with the continuation of prizefighting after human beings have been prohibited from participation in the sport.

Coincidentally, abolitionists had been sharpening their pitchforks and lighting their torches throughout the last couple of years leading up to the night "Steel" was broadcast on October 4, 1963. The boxing world was reeling from the aftershocks of both Estes Kefauver's Senate subcommittee hearings regarding the corruptive underworld influence on prizefighting and two recent in-ring tragedies that claimed the lives of Benny 'Kid' Paret and Davey Moore.

Memorializing Davey Moore's sad fate in verse, Bob Dylan assigned blame for the boxer's death only in part to Moore's opponent, Ultiminio 'Sugar' Ramos. The remainder of the folk balladeer's scorn was directed in equal measure toward the referee, the angry crowd, the cigar-chomping manager, the gamblers, and boxing writers. The fatal bout between Davey Moore and 'Sugar' Ramos had occurred only a little more than six months before the airing of "Steel," with California governor Pat Brown still lobbying for a ban on "this so-called sport." The Vatican even threw its collective peaked hat into the ring, so to speak, when it issued a statement in its official newspaper denouncing boxing as "morally illicit."

These real-world attacks against boxing set the stage for the broadcast of "Steel." Prizefighters who were long in the tooth and down on their luck but who were still willing and able to risk their lives inside the ring despite the odds were among Rod Serling's favorite type of characters to depict. But even he hadn't taken the subject matter into territory anywhere near as far-out as that depicted here.

Matheson's short story is set in 1980 with no specific mention of when the ban on boxing took effect, except for a passage discussing that the Mawling corporation had begun manufacturing android prizefighters as proxies for humans at least as far back as 1967. *The Twilight Zone* episode, a faithful adaptation by Matheson of his own short story, moves the narrative a little closer to the airdate of "Steel." By six years, to be exact, to 1974 as Rod Serling states in his opening narration.

***

In many people's eyes, Lee Marvin is the ultimate badass. The tough guy's idea of a tough guy, he was supposedly expelled from dozens of schools on the grounds of his unrepentantly disruptive behavior. Marvin would later serve in the U.S. Marine Corps during World War II, suffering injuries while engaged in the Battle of Saipan.

Community and summer stock theater led Marvin to Broadway and eventually Hollywood, where he would make his mark courtesy of gritty roles. These largely consisted of parts in westerns and war stories on both the small screen and silver screen, most notably *Dragnet, The Wild One, The Caine Mutiny, M Squad, The Man Who Shot Liberty Valance, The Dirty Dozen, and Paint Your Wagon*. Marvin's appearance in "Steel" was his second trip through The Twilight Zone after having starred in "The Grave," a memorably eerie third season entry.

In this episode, Lee Marvin plays Tim Kelly, an ex-heavyweight contender – "before the law was passed, of course," he stresses–who earned the nickname 'Steel' by virtue of the fact that he had never been knocked down. Richard Matheson referred to 'Steel' Kelly as a "monomaniacal character" in the approximate mold of Captain Ahab, fixated upon a single goal to the detriment of everything else.

Kelly is now the manager of a B-2 android boxer, Battling Maxo (Tipp McClure of *The Untouchables*). Matheson's short story further identifies both Kelly and Maxo as light-heavyweights. In that version of the tale, 'Steel' was once rated number nine, and Maxo is currently ranked fourth thanks to his upset victory over the heavily favored Dimsy the Rock at Madison Square Garden in 1977.

The tenderness Kelly exhibits toward Battling Maxo is the kind typically reserved for a close relation or very dear friend, not unlike the way Army looks after the welfare of Mountain in "Requiem for a Heavyweight." The

85 🏃

same cannot be said of Maxo's mechanic, Pole, who constantly ridicules the squeaky, outdated B-2 as a "steam shovel" and "piece of dead iron."

For what it's worth, unconditional love can sometimes blind one to certain undeniable truths. That appears to be the case here with 'Steel' Kelly, whose sole purpose is to keep Battling Maxo up and running for one more fight, and another, and another still. Kelly cannot see—or more to the point, chooses not to see—how the android is clearly falling to pieces before his very eyes.

Despite his best intentions and undying dedication to Maxo, Steel is complicit in his fighter's swift and unavoidable decline. Pole's emotional detachment, on the other hand, allows him to assess the automaton's situation from a clinical and pragmatic, if harsh, point of view.

Kelly and Pole have lugged Maxo all the way from Philadelphia to Kansas so that their robotic fighter can square off against a B-7 model called The Maynard Flash, winner of seven straight fights (as we're informed in Matheson's short story). The only reason Kelly was able to secure the bout in the first place was because the B-4 originally scheduled as the Flash's opponent was scrapped after being involved in a car wreck. Kelly seemingly tries to convince himself as much as Pole of their chances when he points out that the Flash is just a start model B-7 with the kinks probably not yet worked out of its system.

Underrated character actor Joe Mantell assumes the part of Pole for his second arrival into *The Twilight Zone*, having previously given a standout performance in what was essentially a one-man show called "Nervous Man in a Four Dollar Room."

Nolan, the fight promoter played by Merrit Bohn (who was also the truck driver that accidentally runs down little Maggie in "One for the Angels"), is also less than responsive to Kelly's optimistic appraisal of his broken-down B-2 and just wants a competitive bout for his $500. Maxwell, the promoter's right-hand man preoccupied by counting stacks of cash, is played by Frank London, another return visitor to *The Twilight Zone*, previously appearing in "A Penny for Your Thoughts" starring Dick York.

The locker room looks like a cross between a tool shed and a disorderly high school science lab. Here, the hood which had been covering Maxo's head the entire time is removed to reveal the android's hand-molded facial features and unsettling, vacant eyes. While inventorying and evaluating Maxo's internal damage, Pole worries that his clockwork machinery will be audible all the way in the back row and concludes that they might as well cut their losses and salvage him for parts. Kelly, of course, won't hear of it.

After throwing a left jab at Kelly during their practice session, Maxo experiences a short-circuit. Unfortunately, a replacement part for the sprung gear is no longer available on the open market. With no other options available to collect their pay, Kelly forces Pole into making him appear like a B-2 boxing robot so that he can take Maxo's place. 'Steel' is rolled on coasters toward the ring amidst an assemblage of hecklers shouting, "scrap iron" and "Rattling Maxo!"

In his short story, Richard Matheson describes Maxo's B-7 opponent, The Maynard Flash, as "an impassive Adonis," a nearly perfect specimen. Chuck Hicks, who embodies the robotic Flash, would revisit *The Twilight Zone* soon after as a mover in "Ninety Years Without Slumbering" and had played a boxer on *The Many Loves of Dobie Gillis* in an episode entitled "Requiem for an Underweight Heavyweight," a humorous homage to the recently released movie version of Rod Serling's prizefighting story.

Welterweight contender turned actor and stunt man Johnny Indrisano, who appeared in the movie version of *Requiem for a Heavyweight*, had been brought in to help choreograph the fight scenes. The fact that Marvin and Hicks happened to be old acquaintances was certainly an asset to their performances for this part of the episode. Hicks recalled hitting Marvin for real on a few occasions, but that there were never any hard feelings.

The accidental blows likely resulted from the plastic covering both men's faces, which fogged up inhuman eyes fabricated by *The Twilight Zone* makeup man William Tuttle. After sculpting a layer of clay over a life mask he had taken of each actor, Tuttle cut ping pong balls in half and colored them black to serve as the robotic boxers' eyes and cut pinholes into them for the actors to try their best to see through.

Interestingly, the bout proceeds without the services of a referee. This is because, as Matheson relates in his original story, B models never clinch and once knocked down, are programmed to stay on the canvas, rendering all counts and reprimands completely academic. Mawling was hardwiring their new B-9 prototypes to get back up following a knockdown, which would make for longer, more fan-friendly fights.

After being beaten nearly to death by The Maynard Flash, Kelly lies on the floor of the dressing room with Maxo looming over him like an immobile sentinel while Pole retrieves only half of their promised purse money due to the bout's premature first-round conclusion. Rather than consign Maxo to the scrap heap of chewed-up and spit-out former fighters, quite literally in this case, Kelly vows to use their meager earnings to get back home to Philadelphia and make the necessary repairs which will entitle Maxo to the dubious right to fight another day.

In his closing narration, Rod Serling renders a unanimous decision in favor of humankind's ability to "outfight, outpoint, and outlive" inevitable societal changes.

***

The ever-popular Rock 'Em Sock 'Em Robots hit toy store shelves not too long after the premiere of "Steel" on *The Twilight Zone*. Coincidence? Well, yes, but it's a fun fact to mull over, nevertheless. The Marx Toy Co. encouraged kids to knock the block off The Blue Bomber and The Red Rocket courtesy of hand-controlled levers located just outside the ring. Players would use them to direct a punch to the point of his or her opponent's chin and engage the spring, which would send the plastic prizefighter's head bobbing crazily this way and that.

Rock 'Em Sock 'Em Robots was a mass-produced home version of a mechanical boxing game that had been manufactured decades prior and could be found in penny arcades. Audrey Totter's character Julie wanders around one such venue in 1949's *The Set-Up* rather than subject herself to witnessing her 35-year-old husband Stoker Thompson (Robert Ryan) fight a four-round prelim at the Paradise City Athletic Club. Julie finds momentary distraction and amusement watching teenagers enjoying each other's company until she sees a young couple playing the boxing game, which serves as a painful reminder of her personal dilemma.

Even this was a scaled-down replication of a true-to-life-size boxing game that was fashioned for vacation resorts in the early 1930s. The human competitors would stand outside the ropes and use individual hand wheels to manipulate the mechanical dummies battling inside the ring, which were galvanized by a system of electro-magnets.

***

Former heavyweight champion Jack Dempsey authored an intriguing think-piece in the April 1934 issue of *Modern Mechanix* magazine. Within it, he defiantly stated that, regardless of having been away from the ring for seven years, he would fearlessly square off against "any robot or mechanical man." Dempsey further boasted that he would "tear it to pieces, bolt by bolt" and leave its inner workings scattered all over the canvas.

Breaking down the scientific components to the mental, physical, and technical aspects of prizefighting, Dempsey was adamant that an automa-

ton, no matter how technologically advanced the gadgets and gizmos created by its engineers, was lacking the one element critical to outmatching
their flesh and blood counterparts: brains.

***

In a relevant postscript, Richard Matheson's short story was adapted
into DreamWorks Studios' 2011 blockbuster *Real Steel*. The film starred
Hugh Jackman and grossed $300 million, but it bore little resemblance to
the source material.

Marquess of Queensberry Mayhem in the Night Gallery

CHRISTOPHER BENEDICT

As mentioned earlier, legend has it that Archie Moore was originally cast in the role of Bolie Jackson for *The Twilight Zone's* first season supernatural boxing story, "The Big, Tall Wish." Archie's daughter J'Marie, who won both of her professional bouts under the moniker 'The Lady Mongoose,' confirmed for me that she knows the whole story. She also got to meet Rod Serling once, but she is saving the specifics until she can detail them in her own book. Fair enough.

Though appearing on *The Twilight Zone* didn't pan out for Archie Moore, he would make good on a subsequent opportunity to play a bouncer in a December 1963 episode of NBC's *Chrysler Theatre* written by Serling. Adapted from John O'Hara's short story, "It's Mental Work" tells the gritty tale of a down-on-his-luck bartender (future *Night Gallery* actor Harry Guardino, "The Miracle at Camafeo") attempting to purchase his place of employment from its current owner (Lee J. Cobb of *On the Waterfront* and *12 Angry Men*). The show featured Gena Rowlands and *The Twilight Zone* alums Stanley Adams (who was also in both versions of "Requiem for a Heavyweight") and Larry Blake in addition to the recently retired boxing legend.

Also, if you look closely at the fight posters on the facade of what is supposed to be St. Christopher's Arena as Anthony Quinn's Mountain Rivera meanders down the sidewalk in the *Requiem for a Heavyweight* movie, seeing his own image being covered over, symbolically erasing him, one of the placards is advertising Archie Moore's June 10, 1961 rematch against Giulio Rinaldi at Madison Square Garden.

Rod Serling insisted that a good fighter was a piece of art. Archie Moore was without a doubt one such walking, talking, pugilistic masterpiece whose likeness hangs on a wall in the International Boxing Hall of Fame, even if it does not appear in Washington D.C.'s National Gallery of Art, or Serling's *Night Gallery* for that matter.

***

Airing on NBC between 1969 and 1973, Rod Serling's *Night Gallery* occupies an interesting, transitional time and space in television history. Anthology programs, particularly *Playhouse 90, Studio One, Kraft Theatre, Climax!*, and other prestige series which featured more highbrow fare, had been a huge hit for the few decades prior. They were soon eclipsed in popularity by offerings for younger viewers and morbidly inclined adults, like Serling's *The Twilight Zone, Alfred Hitchcock Presents, The Outer Limits, One Step Beyond*, and *Tales of Tomorrow*. Similarly, the standout shows *Thriller* and *The Veil*, both hosted by Boris Karloff, also gained quite the following.

One by one, they all died quiet, negligibly dignified deaths by the mid-60s. Horror/sci-fi-themed anthology shows wouldn't really see a full-scale resurrection until the 1980s thanks to the likes of *The Hitchhiker, Tales from the Darkside, Ray Bradbury Theater, Amazing Stories, Tales from the Crypt, Monsters*, and short-lived revivals of *Alfred Hitchcock Presents* and *The Twilight Zone*. Given that landscape, some might argue that *Night Gallery* was either ahead of its time, or behind the times, or perhaps stuck in its own weird extra-dimensional limbo.

After five seasons, 156 episodes, and the creative burnout of its prime mover, *The Twilight Zone* experienced a gravitational collapse, like a brilliantly burning star going supernova. Nevertheless, Serling would have been more than willing to keep *The Twilight Zone's* celestial light shining. ABC president Tom Moore offered him a chance at resuscitating the series, only to learn that CBS retained the rights to the name of the show, as they do to this day.

Not to be deterred, Moore suggested the alternate title *Witches, Warlocks, and Werewolves*, borrowing the name from a 1963 paperback collection of horror stories Serling had edited for Bantam. Serling countered with a detailed premise called *Rod Serling's Wax Museum*, but Moore wouldn't budge on the title or concept he had in mind. Serling aired his grievances about the potential of being "hooked into a graveyard every week" in *Variety* magazine, which effectively brought an end to his negotiations with Tom Moore and ABC.

In 1967, Serling published a collection of original novellas entitled *The Season To Be Wary*. He would bring the collection to Sid Sheinberg at Universal, who bought the rights for "something like twelve cents," Rod joked. The Season to Be Wary was comprised of three stories, two of which—"The Escape Route" and "Eyes"—he would soon after adapt into teleplays. He would append an original piece, "The Cemetery," to these two works to complete a trilogy of stand-alone tales for *Night Gallery*, an anthology movie broadcast on November 8, 1969.

The project was given the greenlight at NBC, although their consent came accompanied by demands for multiple alterations to the stories. This wasn't a red flag in and of itself, as Serling had dealt with requests to revise his scripts to one degree or another throughout his writing career. However, as creator and executive producer of *The Twilight Zone*, Serling became accustomed to the type of artistic control he had never enjoyed before. To his ultimate dismay, he would find his authority sorely lacking when it came to *Night Gallery*.

At the root of Serling's problems with the production was a contentious relationship with Jack Laird, a screenwriter, director, and occasional guest actor who cast himself in a handful of *Night Gallery* segments. Laird expressed open disdain for Serling's writing talent but was shrewdly cognizant of the marquee value attached to the name, face, and voice viewers would remember from *The Twilight Zone*. Anne Serling remembers Laird's name being spat out by her father around the house through "gritted teeth."

One of the changes Serling made to the *Night Gallery* pilot film, presumably due to time constraints, removed from the equation a major subplot within his short story. In it, a woebegone boxer, for the benefit of his former manager, consents to selling his eyes to a rich, blind eccentric seeking a clandestine procedure that, if successful, will grant her sight for no more than twelve hours.

Eyes

Curiously, the role of the wealthy, sightless recluse was first presented to Joan Crawford's nemesis and *Whatever Happened to Baby Jane?* costar Bette Davis. She turned the offer down flat based on the presumption that the directorial talents of the college dropout selected to take the reins of "Eyes" would fail to live up to her lofty standards. The unproven novice in question was none other than Steven Spielberg.

Of course, no one knew in 1969 that the "pimply faced kid in an eight-dollar Sears and Roebuck jacket" (in the words of his second assistant director on "Eyes," Ralph Sariego) who strolled onto the set would soon after carve out his rightful place in film history with *Jaws, Close Encounters of the Third Kind, Raiders of the Lost Ark, E.T.*, and more Hollywood blockbusters than you can throw a Mt. Everest-sized pile of money at.

Once *Night Gallery* had been picked up as a series, Spielberg would return to helm another segment called "Make Me Laugh" and, in the process reunite with Tom Bosley after their work together on "Eyes." Spielberg also directed a chipper remake of George Clayton Johnson's maudlin classic "Kick the Can" for *Twilight Zone: The Movie*, which he co-produced with John Landis in 1983.

Joan Crawford, who inherited the part of Claudia Menlo from her rival, was not exactly thrilled to be taking direction from Spielberg either. Not at the outset, anyway. Spielberg admits to being intimidated by the mercurial diva draped in furs and surrounded by a full entourage of personal assistants and sycophants.

Her arrival was augmented by the delivery of both Pepsi and vodka by the case. A notorious drinker, Joan was then married to her fourth and final husband, Al Steele, who was President and CEO of the nation's second most popular cola company. She had been known to insist that Pepsi products be strategically placed within easy sight of the camera lens on the sets of films she had done recently, like William Castle's *Strait-Jacket*.

Despite the initial tension, Spielberg and Crawford came to a mutual understanding that would help smooth over the bumps in the road put in place by the screen legend's burdensome demeanor during production. One common obstacle that Crawford and Spielberg hurdled over together was Rod Serling's formidable dialogue.

Long before shooting started, Crawford was concerned with her ability to realistically convey her lines, complaining that real people didn't speak the way Serling wrote. Many phone calls were placed by Crawford to Rod Serling, much to the writer's annoyance. Knowing full well after a while who to expect on the other end of the line, he would curse under his breath before picking up the phone. Sympathizing with his star, Spielberg patiently helped Crawford find her rhythm while running lines in rehearsal. Spielberg recalled meeting Serling and found him to be encouraging and energetic.

To give a basic rundown of the scenario, Crawford's character Claudia Menlo blackmails her physician, Dr. Frank Heatherton, into performing an experimental procedure whereby he will transplant the optical nerves of a bought-off donor into her eyes. In exchange, she will keep concealed the fact that a young woman with whom Heatherton had an affair had died because of a botched abortion he procured for her.

The surgery is a success, but Menlo's limited number of hours endowed with vision for the first time in her life is ruined when Manhattan is submerged in darkness by a city-wide blackout. She becomes convinced that Heatherton's efforts had failed.

She wakes the next morning to the sight of the rising sun just as the time limit on her vision comes to an end. Stumbling toward the window, Claudia grasps furiously at the glowing orb she knows is there but can no longer see and plunges through the glass, falling to the sidewalk far below.

95

Menlo's donor is Sidney Resnick, a luckless gambler who agrees to her terms. He figures that willingly enduring the rest of his life without the benefit of sight would be preferable to whatever the bookie to whom he owes $9,000 plans to have done to him.

Rod Serling admired and adored Jack Klugman, who had appeared in four *Twilight Zone* episodes, and envisioned him in the role of Resnick. Klugman was unavailable, and the part was offered to fellow *Twilight Zone* veteran Martin Balsam in his stead. He too was unable to fulfill the obligation.

Enter Tom Bosley, best known as *Happy Days* patriarch Howard Cunningham. Crawford and Bosely had costarred a half-dozen years earlier in an episode of *Route 66* called "Same Picture, Different Frame." The only interaction he shared with Crawford on the set of "Eyes" was a "five second phone call" after receiving a brief but cordial letter from her. Bosley surmised that Crawford's disruptive behavior and lengthy absences from the sound stage could be attributed to her being "dead drunk most of the time."

***

Author's note: A word of warning that the following section contains discussion of a story involving sexual assault. If you or someone you know has experienced sexual assault, you are not alone, RAINN's national hotline offers free, confidential support at 800-656-4673 (HOPE).

The original optical donor in Rod Serling's novella of "Eyes," published in the 1967 anthology *The Season To Be Wary*, was Indian Charlie Hatcher. He retains a special place in Serling lore as the last of his broken-down boxers sputtering toward the finish line of life, coasting on fumes and memories that generally fail to qualify as happy ones.

Leaving his Arizona reservation to pursue prizefighting, Indian Charlie racked up 108 fights over sixteen years as a middleweight journeyman. His self-imposed undoing began after a fight one night in his dressing room with a seventeen-year-old girl who was attracted to Charlie, but not old enough to consent. Charlie did time in prison for statutory rape, and the consequences of his actions haunted the rest of his days.

Like consigning an unwanted, worthless antique to the nether regions of a vast, decrepit storehouse, he has tried his best to bury what he refers to as "The Trouble" in the dark recesses of his mind. But "The Trouble" was always there, impossible to ignore. Serling's words imply that Indian Charlie was serving a life sentence inside his own head throughout which he would rattle the bars of his damaged brain cells in a fruitless protest for release.

Hungry, behind on his rent, and wanting desperately to believe that there is still some good in the world, Hatcher accepts an overture from Tony Petrozella. Serling describes Petrozella as "a sometime fight manager, an all-the-time con man" who had years ago parted ways with Indian Charlie with an insult and a slap across the face.

Charlie had won only six of his final eighteen fights and was stopped well inside the distance in the last five. Petrozella had no use for losers. Given the antagonistic nature of their shared past, Hatcher should have known better than to assume that their meeting would culminate in a garden variety job offer.

It turns out Petrozella owes money he doesn't have to a Las Vegas bookie who has given him forty-eight hours to cough up the dough. Otherwise, what little is left of him after his goons get through with their nasty business will be barely enough to spoon into a cup. Rather than do the right thing and accept the consequences, Petrozella hatches a scheme whereby he dupes the gullible Indian Charlie Hatcher into selling his eyes to collect the payoff for himself.

Petrozella takes Hatcher to meet Claudia, but it seems that the resourceful Miss Menlo has done her homework on the potential donor. She deeply upsets Charlie by making him aware of her knowledge pertaining to "The Trouble." The slick-talking Petrozella is able to smooth things out and exits the penthouse overlooking Central Park intoxicated by "thoughts of redheads, fifty-cent cigars, Miami Beach, and the other good things in life."

Back in his dilapidated apartment, Charlie Hatcher communes with the ghost of his father. While doing so, he can see things with a clarity that has eluded him since his youth even though his chosen profession had long since made pulp of his gray matter.

To the apparition floating just outside his apartment window, Charlie vows to "go home." When the ghost asks what he will leave behind, Charlie answers "Only pain, father—only pain" before he hangs himself, silencing his inner demons and leaving Petrozella metaphorically twisting in the wind.

While Serling could not possibly have been aware at the time that "Eyes" would be the last story featuring a prizefighter as the main character that he would ever write, I find it quite revealing that he bookends the tales in this personal subgenre of his in such unapologetically grim fashion—with the suicides of Danny Fales in 1948 and Indian Charlie Hatcher nineteen years later.

The Ring With the Red Velvet Ropes

The *Night Gallery* movie earned Rod Serling the coveted Edgar Allan Poe Award from the Mystery Writers of America, and NBC gave the go-ahead to proceed with the project as a regular series for the network's 1970 Fall schedule. Even though the episode itself was not written by Serling, *Night Gallery* did produce one boxing story.

Screenwriter, director, and documentarian Robert Malcolm Young (who had penned *Nothing But a Man*, starring "The Big, Tall Wish" lead actor Ivan Dixon, and called "action" and "cut" for films like *Short Eyes, One Trick Pony*, and the 1989 boxing movie *Triumph of the Spirit*) wrote the script. He adapted it from the short story "The Ring with the Velvet Ropes" by Edward D. Hoch, a prolific author of whodunits, detective tales, spy novels, mysteries, historical fiction, crime thrillers, and more than 900 short stories.

A 2-to-1 underdog, Jim Figg (Gary Lockwood, of *2001: A Space Odyssey* fame) has just defeated Big Dan Anger (Ji-Tu Cumbuka, later to appear with heavyweight great Ken Norton in *Mandingo* and feature in the *Roots* TV mini-series as well as *Brewster's Millions*) to become the new heavyweight champion of the world. Although it is never mentioned in either the short story or *Night Gallery* teleplay that Figg is a reincarnation of, or distant relation to, boxing's first bareknuckle champion, I have a hard time believing it's strictly a coincidence that they share the same name.

The real James Figg was labeled by Jack Dempsey as the "father of modern boxing." Born in Thames, Oxfordshire in 1695, Figg combined advanced grappling techniques with the fencing maneuvers he had perfected in countless skirmishes to compete in anything-goes prizefights that resembled a primitive and lethal form of mixed martial arts, where the use of swords, truncheons, and quarterstaffs were not only fair game but as commonplace as fisticuffs. Figg, who was the first to refer to pugilism as "the manly art of self- defense," cut his teeth in the boxing booths at fairs across the country. He took on and bested all challengers before going on to claim the Championship of England in 1719.

He is said to have lost only one of 270 bouts, to a pipe-maker named Ned Sutton. Fig had beaten Sutton on a previous occasion, and he would defeat Sutton once again in their rubber match when he incapacitated Sutton by way of a cudgel to the kneecap. Sponsored by the Earl of Peterborough, he opened a boxing academy to train students in the ways of unarmed, hand-to-hand combat, which would come to be called "Figg's fighting."

Exhibitions were staged in an amphitheater that bore his name. In 1722, two women, 'European Championess' Elizabeth Wilkinson and Hannah Hyfield, duked it out in a winner-take-all prizefight while gripping a half-crown in each fist. It was determined that the victor would be the first combatant to force her opponent to drop the coins, thus collecting the spoils while her opponent walked away empty-handed. This would additionally put Figg well ahead of the curve as the first promoter of women's boxing.

Returning to *Night Gallery*. Robert Malcolm Young added minimal supernatural touches to the narrative for "Velvet Ropes," reserved solely for the beginning and end, whereas there were none to be had in Edward D. Hoch's straight-ahead short story about the new titleholder, Jim Figg, being forcibly whisked away the day after winning the belt to the oceanside estate of one Roderick Blanco who introduces himself as the real heavyweight champion.

Naturally, this is news to Figg, who listens to Blanco relate his fantastic tale of having defeated Big Dan Anger—not to mention every other champion who had reigned over the previous decade–in a secret bout held in his basement.

Anger and the others, Blanco tells Figg, were champions in name only after he dispatched them inside his private ring with the velvet ropes, which he admitted was "my one concession to good taste." Now that Figg has beaten Anger in a legitimately sanctioned match, he must defend against Blanco and, additionally, keep the real champion's identity and whereabouts under wraps.

The son of a rich man who "died in an asylum," Blanco must publicly refrain from fighting until he turns thirty-five in order to cash in his considerable trust fund. If he is found out, he loses it all. To illustrate the gravity of the situation, Roderick's wife Sandra warns Figg that the loose-lipped referee of her husband's bout with Big Dan Anger was run over by a car after drunkenly blurting out things he had no business making public. Left with no alternative, Figg agrees to a fight officiated by real-life referee Frankie Van, who was also the third man in the ring for the Bolie Jackson vs. Joey Consiglio bout in "The Big, Tall Wish."

In Edward D. Hoch's short story, Blanco floors Figg twice in the sixth round, the point at which Roderick had put Anger away in their contest. Jim nevertheless survives the onslaught and catches Blanco with his guard down in the eighth just long enough to pepper him with a four-punch combination that ends the fight. A sore loser, Roderick threatens to shoot Figg and allows him to leave only under strict orders of secrecy and a gentleman's agreement to a return bout. Once returned to the outside world, however, Jim announces his retirement before receiving a phone call from Sandra Blanco. She informs him that Roderick couldn't live with the knowledge that he would never defeat one champion and hanged himself from one of his boxing ring's velvet ropes.

The *Night Gallery* episode gave Hoch's story a twist, and it goes like this: Figg turns Roderick over after knocking him out and sees, to his horror, that Blanco has immediately decomposed in the center of the ring. He is told that the ancient Roderick Blanco held the title since defeating Jem Mace in 1861 and had successfully defended it against all other champions until that night. "Winner take all," Blanco's wife Sandra tells Figg as she entwines her arm with his and leads the new champion off to begin his reign.

Roderick Blanco is portrayed by the quintessential square-jawed man's-man Chuck Connors. A two-sport standout, Connors played portions of two seasons with the Boston Celtics, becoming the first professional basketball player to shatter a backboard, before switching to baseball and putting in time with both the Brooklyn Dodgers and Chicago Cubs. He isn't known to have boxed, but one report alleges that he and comedian Joey Bishop staged an impromptu exhibition between bouts during a December 10, 1970, Olympic Auditorium card. The evening was headlined by a grudge match between former stablemates Mando Ramos and Raul Rojas, which Ramos won by KO in the sixth round.

As for the shenanigans involving Connors and Bishop, a website dedicated to the actor alleges that it concluded "when a burly character leaped into the ring and bear-hugged Connors off the floor." The identity of the third participant is unknown. A nifty story, if only it were true.

Rick Farris, a former fighter who is now president and co- founder of the West Coast Boxing Hall of Fame, opened the show on the evening in question with a four-round win on points over Antonio Villanueva. Although Rick told me that Connors was indeed sitting ringside, he said that Chuck was not even interviewed for the televised portion of the event by famed broadcaster Jim Healy, as was Connie Stevens, and most definitely "did not step into the ring that night." Farris doesn't remember Bishop, who was "a regular at the Olympic," being there on that occasion, although Burt Reynolds, Peter Falk, and Robert Goulet were. "Aileen [Eaton, the popular Olympic Auditorium promoter] loved Hollywood ringside, not in the ring," Rick stressed.

Gary Lockwood had fond memories of filming the fight scenes with Connors, recalling the star of *The Rifleman* and *Branded* as "very professional" and that working out the footwork and pulled punches were "no problem." For what it's worth, Lockwood knew his way around the ring from his days as an amateur boxer. With that said, both the choreography and cinematography of the bout between Connors and Lockwood leave a lot to be desired. The same can be said, unfortunately, about the episode. The interaction between Lockwood and Joan Van Ark (*Knots Landing*) as Sandra Blanco, for example, was supposed to be charged with sexual tension that flatlines miserably.

Likewise, the otherworldly ambience originating with scriptwriter Robert Malcolm Young and made manifest under Jeannot Szwarc's direction (Szwarc helmed nineteen *Night Gallery* segments) is pronounced dead on arrival, except for one nice touch.

Blanco's reveal takes a little longer to get to than in the short story, and his offscreen presence is implied by the distant echoes of a speedbag being struck repeatedly while Figg and Sandra converse. As Jim and Sandra depart at the end of the episode, Roderick's body has mysteriously disappeared from the ring. At that point, there is a reprise of the same sound effect.

Young's adaptation of Hoch's short story does away with Figg's fiancée Sue and an always-eager-for-a-scoop sportswriter named Connie Claus. While Sue was no more than a peripheral character who isn't missed much, Claus would have, in my opinion, been a welcome addition to the episode. Even so, neither character's presence would have improved a rather pedestrian entry into the *Night Gallery*.

***

After its cancellation, Rod Serling expressed sincere regret about the "uncommentative" quality of *Night Gallery*, which ran for three seasons before airing for the final time on May 27, 1973. Even if Serling's supernatural follow-up to *The Twilight Zone* failed to live up to the high bar set by its predecessor both creatively and critically, *Night Gallery* remains a fan favorite.

CHRISTOPHER BENEDICT

In the last few years, the series has received deluxe treatment. Kino Lorber released Blu-ray box sets for all three seasons of the show. *Night Gallery* historians Scott Skelton and Jim Benson, meanwhile, produced a pair of museum-quality books: *Rod Serling's Night Gallery: The Art of Darkness*, which places an emphasis on Tom Wright's macabre paintings that Rod Serling would use to introduce each segment, and an immensely updated and expanded edition of the co-authors' 1998 episode guide, *Night Gallery: An After Hours Tour*.

ROUND
9

Keep Punching

Rod Serling's writings, even when adapted from pre-existing sources, were always uniquely his own. Whether it's the unmistakably verbose dialogue spoken by his characters, the compassion and pathos with which he treated the most deserving among them, or the ironic twists of fate that bedeviled others, a script that originated from the imagination and typewriter of Rod Serling was like no other. His stories have not only stood the test of time but remained critically relevant to both society and the entertainment industry. Boxing, being our specific topic of discussion, is certainly no exception.

For instance, Serling's literary fingerprints can be detected throughout the scripts for the first two *Rocky* movies. Just as Rod had done with Mountain in both versions of *Requiem for a Heavyweight*, Sylvester Stallone borrowed elements from a handful of different real-life pugilists to patch together the character of Rocky Balboa.

There was 'The Brockton Blockbuster' Rocky Marciano, the unbeaten bulldozer of a heavyweight champion whose name, crude, hammer-handed fighting style, and shared heritage Stallone bequeathed onto 'The Italian Stallion.' When we are first introduced to a financially and existentially struggling Balboa, a poster of Marciano hangs prominently yet haphazardly in his ramshackle apartment. It serves Rocky as a tangible reminder to pick yourself up and keep punching no matter how many times life knocks you down.

There was Philadelphia's own Joe Frazier, the main nemesis to Muhammad Ali. Frazier implemented a training regimen that involved punching the slabs of beef hanging in the meat-packing plant where he worked and running the steps of Fairmount Park to build his stamina. Looking fashionable in a lime green leisure suit, Smokin' Joe is brought into the ring and introduced to the crowd before the climactic title fight between Rocky Balboa and Apollo Creed in the first film.

There was 'The Bayonne Bleeder' Chuck Wepner, the debt collector for a Jersey bookie and hard-luck, thin-skinned heavyweight contender. His 1975 million-to-one title shot at Muhammad Ali inspired Stallone to have Apollo pluck an unknown club fighter out of obscurity for the chance of a lifetime. Chuck also got dumped over the top rope by Andre the Giant in a boxer vs. wrestler attraction at Shea Stadium before the closed-circuit broadcast of the mixed match between Ali and Antonio Inoki. Perhaps this was on Stallone's mind when he scripted the Rocky vs. Thunderlips (Hulk Hogan) exhibition in *Rocky III*? Sly denied it in a deposition when he was sued by Wepner, although he later agreed to an out of court settlement. Wepner, who we will circle back around to shortly, still refers to himself to this day as 'The Real Rocky'.

Of course, Rocky Balboa also has more than a little in common with Mountain McClintock/Rivera. Sharing many of the same personality traits, neither of them fit the mold of the typical desensitized pug. Compassionate and almost childlike in their simplicity, both Mountain and Rocky are naive to a fault. They are each susceptible to backstabbers and pillagers who exploit their kindness as a weakness. In turn, Mountain and Rocky seek out the nurturing trust of a chosen few.

Trainer Mickey Goldmill is as cantankerous as old-school palookas come, but his devotion to Rocky is undeniable. Their mutually beneficial bond is reminiscent of the one between Army and Mountain in *Requiem for a Heavyweight*, more akin to father and son than simply trainer and boxer. Mickey is deftly performed by the incomparable Burgess Meredith who played iconic characters in *The Twilight Zone*, was the villainous Penguin in the 1966 *Batman* television show and stepped into Rod Serling's shoes by narrating *Twilight Zone: The Movie* in 1983.

In need of more soulful companionship, Rocky frequents the pet shop across the street from Mickey's gym not only to pick up food for his turtles Cuff and Link, but to joke around with the shy, unassuming, socially awkward Adrian, to whom he has taken a liking. As mismatched a pair as they might look to the naked eye, the bespectacled wallflower and the wiseguy with the relaxed brain are outcasts who don't easily fit in with others but fit perfectly well together.

The same was largely true of Grace and Mountain in *Requiem* even though their relationship isn't given time to develop, much less room to breathe, the way Rocky and Adrian's love story flourished throughout three decades' worth of movies. Even so, Grace's sympathy toward the proud but downtrodden almost heavyweight champion of the world who stumbles into her employment office develops into genuine affection. The getting-to-know-you scene where Grace and Mountain share a conversation and a beer at the hotel bar and begin to let their defenses down around one another is somewhat reminiscent of Rocky and Adrian's Thanksgiving night date at the ice-skating rink.

After 111 fights, Mountain is forced into retirement after getting knocked out by Cassius Clay when a commission-appointed doctor reveals the presence of damage that could lead Mountain to lose his vision. At the beginning of *Rocky II*, Balboa is hospitalized following his split decision loss to Apollo Creed (who, coincidentally, was based on Muhammad Ali) and issued a similarly grievous warning about the risk to his eyesight if he continues fighting.

Rocky decides to step away from boxing (for a very limited time, it goes without saying). In the meantime, he is belittled by a director after botching an audition for a TV commercial. It is more harsh but still similar in nature to Mountain being rudely dismissed when applying for a job as a movie theater usher in *Requiem*. Like Mountain, Rocky is left with little choice but to endure a crushing blow to his pride by walking through the doors of an employment agency.

Thematically, *Rocky III* remains mostly grounded in reality and is a very serviceable sequel to the first two entries. That said, Stallone's characterization of Rocky Balboa begins the unwelcomed transformation from a relatable everyman into a musclebound superhero ripped from the pages of a comic book and projected onto a movie screen. Case in point: *Rocky IV*, which dives headlong into far campier territory with Balboa single-handedly, and laughably, fighting the Cold War in a boxing ring. The fifth film overcorrects its steer back toward the grittier aesthetics that made the franchise so beloved and believable in the first place. The result is a messy car crash of a movie that should have put a merciful end to the series. But Rocky lived to fight another day in yet another movie, of course, with any resemblance to Mountain Rivera having long since eroded.

***

No boxing movie comes charging out of the corner swinging with as much violent fury as *Raging Bull*. Martin Scorsese's 1980 masterpiece hits hardest at former middleweight champion Jake LaMotta, who is presented unsparingly as both the protagonist and antagonist of his own biopic. This should come as little surprise to anyone who has read LaMotta's brutally honest autobiography of the same name that served as the primary source material for Scorsese's film and at the end of which Jake emerges looking even worse by comparison.

While punching the walls of his prison cell towards the end of the movie, Robert DeNiro's woeful and seemingly repentant LaMotta bellows that he's not an animal. That's certainly debatable, but one thing for sure is that there is a clear moral divide between the 'Raging Bull' and Mountain McClintock/Rivera. There is the one scene in the film version of *Requiem* where Anthony Quinn's Mountain drags Grace onto the hotel bed with him. Before going too far, he comes to his senses and remorsefully sends her away. The fact that he is clearly ashamed of the momentary loss of self-control over his primal urges stands in stark contrast against LaMotta's vicious cycle of repeated verbal and physical abuse of his wives in *Raging Bull*, not to mention in real life.

This difference between Mountain and Jake might leave you wondering about the common ground between LaMotta and Serling's boxers. There isn't much, but it's there. For one thing, although DeNiro and Joe Pesci's Jake and Joey LaMotta obviously have flesh and blood counterparts, their volatile sibling rivalry calls to mind a similar sort of animosity that exists between fictional brothers Rory and Steve Garrity in Rod Serling's 1955 boxing program "Garrity's Sons."

There is a more direct connection, though. A Serling Easter egg can be found by eagle-eyed viewers toward the end of *Raging Bull*, which is bookended by a grossly overweight LaMotta rehearsing his nightclub schtick in a dressing room. The movie concludes with Jake reciting Marlon Brando's "I coulda been a contender" oration from *On the Waterfront* before he's given the five-minute warning by Scorsese playing a stagehand.

A sign outside the Barbizon-Plaza advertises that evening's show with the enticement that LaMotta will be performing the works of Paddy Chayefsky, Rod Serling, Shakespeare, Budd Schulberg, and Tennessee Williams. Though we're unfortunately not treated to it on camera, it's safe to assume that Serling's contribution to Jake's lounge act would have been a soliloquy from *Requiem for a Heavyweight*.

***

Author's note: A word of warning that the following section contains discussion of suicide and intimate partner violence.

As mentioned previously, the first and last of Rod Serling's boxing writings both conclude with the suicide of their respective protagonists, Danny Fales from his 1948 short story "The Good Right Hand" and Indian Charlie Hatcher in the novella "Eyes." Sadly, former and even active boxers taking their own lives, seriously contemplating suicide, or dying under questionable circumstances exist as realities that are far from irregular.

Some were ill-equipped to cope with the debilitating effects of physical and/or mental health issues. Others spiraled downward due to drug and alcohol addiction or felt compelled to indulge a dangerous impulse for violence that could not be satisfied within the boxing ring. In certain cases, struggling pugilists faced all of the above.

One common denominator is the inescapable truth that absorbing an untold number of blows to the head causes varying degrees of irreversible brain damage, the most severe of which can be responsible for erratic behavior and destructive tendencies acted out against intimate familiars as well as oneself. Below are just a few examples.

We'll start with Johnny Indrisano, the 1920s and 30s welterweight scrapper who had a brief cameo in the movie version of *Requiem for a Heavyweight* and choreographed the *Twilight Zone* boxing match between Lee Marvin and Chuck Hicks for "Steel." Despondent for many years following a divorce from the mother of his only child, Indrisano lost his lingering battle with depression and hung himself on his daughter's birthday in his San Fernando Valley home in 1968.

'The Illinois Thunderbolt' Billy Papke, a second-generation boxer, won the world middleweight title from the great Stanley Ketchel but lost it right back to him two months after. He later made ends meet as a host for a Los Angeles café once owned by former heavyweight contender 'Fireman' Jim Flynn. Papke met his demise in a tragic 1936 murder/suicide, having first shot his ex-wife Edna to death because of her refusal to reconcile with him. He left behind three sons.

Norman Selby, originator of what he coined "the corkscrew punch," fought somewhere between a hundred to two hundred times (mileage varies depending on the source) under the name Charles 'Kid' McCoy from 1891 to 1912. Some of his subsequent professions were as a silent film actor, diamond dealer, detective, and fire chief. Having tied the knot a grand total of ten times himself, McCoy was convicted of murdering a married woman with whom he had become involved. Three years after being freed from prison, McCoy swallowed a large dose of sleeping pills and never woke up. He wrote in his suicide note that he "could not stand the world's madness."

Jock McAvoy was a British Boxing Board of Control and Commonwealth middleweight champion who compiled a career record of 132-14-1 (88 KOs) between 1927 and 1945 and held the BBBofC light-heavyweight belt. He was confined to a wheelchair after being stricken with polio in 1951, having already toiled through diphtheria and a broken neck. Twenty years later, suffering from chronic depression and insomnia, he ended his torment on his 63rd birthday by overdosing on barbiturates.

Venezuelan sensation Edwin Valero began his pro boxing career with eighteen consecutive first-round knockouts. He stopped each one of his 27 opponents inside the distance en route to becoming a two-division world champion, with a potential super-clash with Manny Pacquiao looming on the horizon. Valero was even more cold-blooded outside the ring than he was between the ropes, however, and overwhelming his system with alcohol, cocaine, crack, and ecstasy certainly didn't help. He murdered his wife Jennifer in a hotel room and later hung himself using his sweatpants in his prison cell in 2010.

The deaths of Freddie Mills, Randy Turpin, Arturo Gatti, and Alexis Arguello were all attributed to suicide, but enough circumstantial evidence exists in each instance to cast serious doubt onto the official findings. Mills and Turpin were very likely the victims of mob hits. Meanwhile, it is strongly believed that Gatti was killed by his wife following a heated argument and Arguello the target of a political assassination in his native Nicaragua, with each one of the murders listed above all staged to look like suicides.

The betting odds were stacked as high as the roof of the Tulsa Convention Center against Michael Bentt the night he won the WBO world heavyweight championship in 1993 by virtue of a stunning first-round knockout of Tommy Morrison. Even so, this wasn't the culmination of a lifelong dream. A four-time New York Golden Gloves champion who missed out on two chances to become a 1988 Olympian (losing to Ray Mercer in the trials and box-offs in an attempt to make the U.S. squad and refusing a spot on the Jamaican team because it would mean forfeiting his American citizenship), Bentt had no aspirations toward turning pro but was forced into it by his domineering father. He suffered such anguish over being knocked out in the first round of his first professional fight that he found himself biting down on the barrel of a gun one night. Fortunately, Michael chose not to pull the trigger, though he grudgingly continued his boxing career until being beaten into a coma by, and losing his heavyweight title to, Herbie Hide in his first defense. Bentt defied the odds again by living through the ordeal and becoming a beloved actor and trainer. Bentt's story is poignantly told in the Netflix series, *Losers*, in the Season One episode, "The Miscast Champion."

I could go on, but you get the picture and it's not a pretty one. Suicide is an uncomfortably thorny topic but makes for a conversation that is crucial to bring to light. Clint Eastwood's Oscar-winning *Million Dollar Baby* opened such a controversial dialogue upon its release in 2004, one that continues to be had two decades later.

Million Dollar Baby is screenwriter Paul Haggis' adaptation of the short story collection *Rope Burns*, written by former cut man Jerry Boyd under the pen name F.X. Toole. Both tell of the evolving relationship between female boxer Maggie Fitzgerald (portrayed by Hilary Swank, who was prepared for the role by real-life fighter Maureen Shea) and her reluctant trainer, Frankie Dunn (Eastwood). Eddie 'Scrap-Iron' Dupris (Morgan Freeman), a battle-scarred veteran of the prize ring, helps the two to connect. Dupris may be blind in one eye, but he retains the uncanny ability to look more deeply and see with greater clarity than most, who are either unable or unwilling to do so.

From taking home the uneaten food left behind by patrons of the diner where she waits tables so she can save money to buy her own speed bag to fighting for the world title, Maggie's rags to riches story does not have a happy ending. She is paralyzed as a result of being sucker punched after the bell by Billie 'The Blue Bear' Osterman and striking her neck on the stool Frankie has placed in her corner for the rest period between rounds and can't pull away in time as he watches Maggie sink toward the canvas in stunned disbelief.

Maggie loses her leg as well as her sense of self-worth during her long hospitalization and asks Frankie to put her out of her misery, like her father had done for the family dog when she was a little girl. Her request for him to perform a mercy killing places Dunn, who has already been wallowing in a crisis of faith and Catholic guilt, in conflict between adherence to his strict moral code and his devotion to the young woman he has grown to love as a surrogate daughter. Whether it means leaving her to suffer or having to let her go, Frankie is mired in the quandary of being a willing participant to either terrible possibility.

Just as he adamantly declined to train Maggie and allow her into his life to begin with, he refuses her appeal for euthanasia. However, his mind is made up after she bites through her tongue in a desperate attempt to bleed to death. Late one night, Frankie sneaks into her hospital room, where he turns off the ventilator, removes her breathing tube, and administers a fatal dose of adrenaline. Prior to doing so, Frankie explains to Maggie in hushed tones exactly what is going to happen. He then finally reveals to her that the Gaelic nickname "Mo Cuishle" he had taken to calling her means "my darling, my blood" and gives her a heartbreaking kiss goodbye.

F.X. Toole had been a cornerman for amateur national champion Juli Crocket, who fought professionally on three occasions—winning each time—before transitioning to a career as a musician and playwright that she happily continues to pursue to this day. It was Crockett, Toole said in interviews given shortly before his death in 2002, who he used as the foundation for Maggie Fitzgerald in his short story "Million \$\$\$ Baby."

To my knowledge, Toole never made mention of a woman named Katie Dallam. Be that as it may, there are too many eerie similarities between her and Hillary Swank's character to go ignored. Both Katie and Maggie came from Missouri, grew up in near poverty, didn't begin boxing until their 30s, and had their careers cut short by in-ring tragedies.

With only six weeks of formal training and one Tough Woman contest under her belt, an ill-prepared Dallam stepped between the ropes for her 1996 professional boxing debut against future three-division world champion Sumya 'The Island Girl' Anani. Katie's trainer Joe Gallegos threw in the towel a little more than halfway through round four, but the damage had already been done. In just over seven minutes, Dallam was battered by more than one hundred and fifty punches from Anani and returned fewer than forty.

Complaining of a headache back in her dressing room, Katie vomited and lost consciousness. She was rushed to a nearby hospital, where she underwent three hours of emergency surgery to relieve the hematoma on her brain caused by alarming leakage from the shredded blood vessels. Like Maggie in *Million Dollar Baby*, Dallam spent quite some time in a state of physical paralysis and suicidal despair. Unlike her fictional counterpart, however, Katie survived her nightmare and took up painting as a way of expressing the innermost thoughts she could seldom find the words to articulate.

Million Dollar Baby's villainous Billie 'The Blue Bear' was played by undefeated Hall of Fame boxer Lucia Rijker, who also choreographed the fight sequences. A longtime Buddhist, Rijker is the exact antithesis of the unmerciful character who crippled Maggie. In a bizarre 2013 example of life imitating art imitating life, Rijker was working the corner of her protégé Diana Prazak, who knocked out defending WBC super-featherweight champion Frida Wallberg to win the title. During the post-fight celebration, Lucia sprang into action when Wallberg collapsed on the way back to her corner and instinctively called for medical attention. Frida was conveyed to Karolinska Institutet near Stockholm and had a severe brain hemorrhage caused by a fourth-round clash of heads successfully repaired. Wallberg awoke from a medically induced coma and has recovered wonderfully, thanks in large part to the quick-thinking and benevolent actions of Lucia Rijker, for whom Frida is profoundly grateful.

Author's Note: If you are experiencing persistent feelings of anxiety and despair or having suicidal thoughts, please reach out to a trusted friend or family member, or dial 988 to speak with a mental healthcare professional at the Suicide and Crisis Lifeline.

***

Let's return to Chuck Wepner, whose life story has been given the cinematic treatment on two occasions—well, three if we're counting *Rocky*. The less said about 2019's godawful *The Brawler* the better. But three years earlier, Liev Schreiber, a lifelong fight fan and narrator of countless HBO boxing documentaries, assumed the starring role in *Chuck* and delivered a superb performance. Don't let the mundane title fool you. *Chuck* (originally called *The Bleeder*, a nickname Wepner never cared for and released as such in certain regions) is imaginative, entertaining, and infinitely rewatchable.

With regard to Rod Serling, Wepner, who is still alive and punching at the age of 86, is a huge fan of *Requiem for a Heavyweight*. Fittingly, there are several references to it in *Chuck*. He relates to viewers, through Schreiber's voiceover in an early scene, that the movie breaks his heart every time because he sees a reflection of himself in Mountain Rivera.

Chuck lies in bed watching *Requiem* on TV after finding out from his trainer and manager Al Braverman (Ron Perlman) that he's earned a title shot at then-heavyweight champion George Foreman by mounting a comeback in his previous fight to knock out 'The Stormin' Mormon' Terry Hinke, one of Big George's chief sparring partners. With his arm around his wife Phyllis (Elisabeth Moss), Wepner quotes Mountain's speech to Grace about not being a freak, a punk, or someone with, in Grace's words, "special problems" in synch with Anthony Quinn.

As fate would have it, Muhammad Ali shocked the world once again by knocking out the seemingly invincible George Foreman in their Rumble in the Jungle, regaining the heavyweight title and potentially spoiling Wepner's status as a potential contender. However, Don King, being shrewdly aware that Black versus White in the ring equaled green in the cash register, hyped Wepner as the latest "Great White Hope" looking to dethrone an African American heavyweight champion.

Despite a questionable occurrence in the ninth round which saw Ali hit the deck courtesy of what initially appeared to be a clean body shot, but the champ later argued that it was an errant boot placed atop his own followed by a shove (a still photo from one particular angle seems to back this up), Chuck was badly beaten and eventually stopped with less than twenty seconds remaining in the fight. Wepner might not have lasted the full fifteen-round distance with Ali like Rocky did with Apollo, but he came damn close and was happy to tell anyone within earshot all about it.

Later, Chuck seeks solace in a neighborhood bar after losing to Ali and causing yet another rift with Phyllis. He shamelessly flirts with Linda (portrayed by Naomi Watts), the plucky bartender and next Mrs. Wepner. Ironically, Schreiber and Watts had been in a long-term relationship to that point but split up soon after *Chuck* premiered at the Venice Film Festival. In any event, Linda playfully brings a bigheaded Wepner down a peg by taunting him about stepping on Ali's foot to precipitate the knockdown, to which Chuck responds with Mountain's self-affirming boast in *Requiem* that he was almost heavyweight champion of the world. Linda charms and disarms Chuck at the same time by replying that he's no Mountain Rivera.

A liquor salesman who didn't shy away from imbibing whenever the mood struck, Wepner starts to party especially hard after the success of Sylvester Stallone's Academy Award-winning boxing movie, becoming engrossed in his alter ego of 'The Real Rocky' to the detriment of his marriage, his relationship with his daughter, and his own welfare. In a show of goodwill, Sylvester Stallone offers Chuck a role in the sequel as Rocky's sparring partner, a bruiser from Jersey named Chink Weber.

The only lines Wepner is interested in running with his enabling friend John Stoehr (played by standup comedian Jim Gaffigan) and their ready and willing gal pals the night before his audition isn't in the script he's been given to study but in the baggie of cocaine that is poured out and cut up on the poolside table. Wepner once again recites Mountain's employment office monologue from *Requiem*, this time while naked, coked up, and clutching a half-empty vodka bottle on the edge of a diving board. He regales his captive audience with his impression of Sonny Liston in the second Ali fight by taking a plunge off the deep end.

* * *

"The Sixteen-Millimeter Shrine" was *The Twilight Zone*'s fourth episode, written by Rod Serling and first broadcast on October 23, 1959. In it, Ida Lupino plays Barbara Jean Trenton, an aging Hollywood actress unable to cope with the fact that time has cruelly robbed her of her youth, her vitality, her career, and people close to her. She eventually consigns herself to the fate of being quite literally trapped in the past.

In a November 18, 2024, article for the Boxing Scene website titled "Submitted For Your Approval: Mike Tyson and *The Twilight Zone*," writer Kieran Mulvaney drew an interesting parallel between Barbara Jean and the 58-year-old boxer's ill-advised circus sideshow of a comeback fight against YouTuber turned prizefighter Jake Paul.

"The Sixteen-Millimeter Shrine" refers to the private screening room in which Barbara Jean Trenton sequesters herself, constantly rerunning films made in the prime of her life that allow her to exist in a celluloid dream-world of suspended animation. Mike Tyson, on the other hand, shared fleeting glimpses of his training sessions on social media wherein his hand speed, punching power, footwork, and head movement appeared comparable to days gone by when he had once earned the reputation of 'The Baddest Man on the Planet,' allowing more than a few fans to buy into the delusion that Mike somehow discovered the trick to turning back the hands of the clock as forcibly as he had tried to snap Francois Botha's arm in two during their bout twenty-five years earlier.

Everyone who tuned in to the sad, overhyped spectacle on Netflix is well aware that it didn't exactly turn out that way. Tyson was barely ambulatory, a far cry from recapturing the lightning in a bottle possessed by the 20-year-old version of himself who almost inconceivably knocked down Trevor Berbick three times with one punch to become the youngest heavyweight champion in boxing history. In what could be described as a *Twilight Zone* type of cosmic justice, it appeared as though Father Time had personally ruled against Tyson and cursed him for the sins of his past. Kind of like what Jake LaMotta says to his brother Joey in the locker room after losing a disputed decision to Sugar Ray Robinson in *Raging Bull* about having done so many bad things, maybe he was jinxed, and it was all coming back to him.

Tyson's return to the ring recalls another *Twilight Zone* episode penned by Rod Serling, season five's "A Short Drink From a Certain Fountain." This story saw a desperate man named Harmon Gordon (played by Patrick O'Neal) try to satisfy the whims of his vigorous young wife Flora (Ruta Lee) by experimenting with a serum that reverses the aging process. In the curious case of Harmon Gordon, the treatments prove to be effective. But too much so, as he rapidly regresses all the way back to infancy.

Mike Tyson isn't the first boxer who has tempted fate by taking a generous gulp from the fountain of youth. Rest assured he won't be the last. Some fighters have even accomplished great things in the twilight rounds of their boxing lives. But for every success story like Archie Moore, George Foreman, Alicia Ashley, or Bernard Hopkins, there are an inordinate number of melancholy anecdotes that feature the likes of James J. Jeffries, Joe Louis, Muhammad Ali, and Larry Holmes, who overstayed their welcome with predictably disagreeable results.

There can be a fine line between fairy tales and cautionary tales in the boxing world even more often than in *The Twilight Zone.*

ROUND 10

Rod Serling:
A Writer and a Fighter

Suffice it to say, Rod Serling, a chronicler of the myriad dimensions of the human condition, found many aspects of boxing objectionable. It is tough to see a sport that demands a life and death commitment from its participants treat them with such utter indifference after they have reached their sell-by date, no longer valuable as a tradeable commodity.

Major League Baseball, the NBA, the NFL, and the NHL all have players associations that advocate for the physical and financial protection of their athletes. No comparable agency or entity provides a similar form of oversight in professional boxing.

In 2000, the Muhammad Ali Boxing Reform Act became Federal law as an amendment to the Professional Boxing Safety Act, which Congress passed four years prior. Its well-intentioned objective to protect fighters from being taken advantage of by managers, promoters, and sanctioning bodies looked good on paper. The vaguery of some of its proposals, however, has unfortunately left them open to interpretation. This is compounded by the fact that there is no sole governing body to enforce the provisions, instead leaving judgments to be handed down by individual state athletic commissions on a case-by-case basis.

Upon retirement, prizefighters don't get a goodbye party and a gold watch, much less a pension, a 401k, and an invitation to old timers' day. A select few with an impressive enough résumé will have their moment in the sun on the dais at the Boxing Hall of Fame, where they will deliver a thank you speech, receive a commemorative ring, and have their plaque assume a place of honor on a wall in the museum among the upper crust of their fistic peers.

It is always great to see former boxers reacclimate to life outside the ring ropes, making personal appearances and signing endorsement deals, reuniting and sharing war stories with former rivals, becoming commentators or trainers, or, at the very least, happily making up for lost time with their families and loved ones. This seems to be more common now than in the past, but it is still all too often the apparent exception to the rule. For other former fighters, there will be financial hardships, alcohol and/or drug addiction, criminal activity and incarceration, bouts with clinical depression and suicidal ideation, abuse or self-harm, and the troubling onset of memory lapses, slurred speech, and involuntary tremors.

You will frequently hear misguided talk of comebacks, lamentable rumors, some of which actually get followed through on. Maybe it's because they're not prepared to succeed in any vocation outside the hurt business.

119

Or perhaps it's that they find it nearly impossible to exist without the validation of one-on-one competition, the roar of the crowd, the fans slapping them on the back and calling them "champ," asking for their autograph.

It could be that a fighter's accumulated winnings were squandered, lost to bad business ventures, or misappropriated by managers, promoters, or even family members. Boxers have ended up living in homeless shelters or out on the streets, something seen often enough to bring anyone to tears. Some of these unfortunate ex-boxers who fall on hard times are left to rely on charitable outreach from fans or fellow fighters. Others are either too proud to accept what they see as handouts or are forgotten about by the public to the point where they live largely off the grid. Those without any support must face the unenviable task of toughing things out on their own with minimal resources at their disposal.

With all of that in mind, what compelled Serling to proclaim, "I've always liked fighting and fighters"? A competitive spirit was embedded in Serling's DNA, and this manifested itself not just throughout his writing career but in youthful athletic endeavors. Serling himself had boxed in the Army while attending jump school during basic training. I would venture to guess that boxing's primal challenge to an individual's fight or flight instincts appealed to Serling immensely. A proponent of racial equality, champion of the oppressed, and voice to the voiceless, it should come as no surprise that Serling admired Joe Louis as much as he did. Not simply because "The Brown Bomber" carried a fivefingered detonator in his right glove, but because of the way Louis represented both the boxing community and the Black community with a softspoken yet unmistakable dignity.

In the final analysis, the way Rod Serling saw it, great reward was earned only through the taking of great risk by the writer as well as the prizefighter. Boxing and writing are ultimately solitary pursuits. Serling likely drew many parallels between these two disciplines that correspond in unique and meaningful ways.

Serling candidly confessed in his last interview that writing so much for so long had tired him out and that he no longer enjoyed the process, except when it manifested itself effortlessly. The constant questioning of his own worth, which was a byproduct of rejection as much as self-reflection, had also taken its toll on him over time.

I have no doubt that all boxers who have endured the loftiest highs and loneliest lows of physical, mental, and emotional endurance while chasing a dream sometimes only they themselves are able to envision can relate to

Serling's mercilessly honest sentiments. The innumerable hours spent in preparation and monastic isolation, the anxiety and self-doubt, the fleeting sensations of elation or grandeur, the weight of external pressures to deliver the goods, the alternating moments of insurmountable struggle and effortless cruising as if on autopilot, and, ultimately, the pride in having accomplished the task at hand—knowing full well that, win, lose, or draw, you left everything you had to give on the blood-splattered canvas or the typewritten paper—are what define the shared experience.

For both the boxer and the author, it all comes down to perseverance. In the quest to win the respect of one's peers in equal measure to achieving the respect of oneself. To power through indescribable pain and suffer the torment of self-afflicted unease. To lie down at night comforted by the thought that you have won some victory not just for yourself, but maybe even for humanity.

Rod Serling saw and shared the humanity of the marginalized, the broken, and the dispossessed. The underdog is always front and center in his stories. By unfailingly fighting the good fight, Rod Serling's writings and ideals, his warmth and humility, his determination and decency will live on forever.

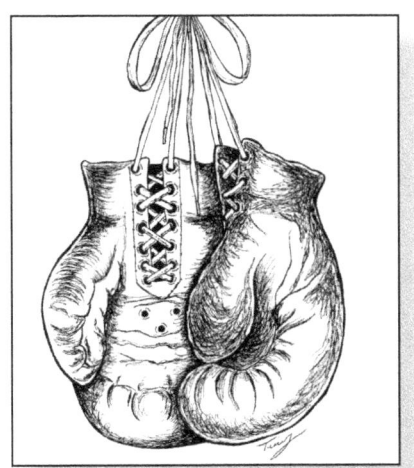

Suggestions for Further Reading or Viewing:

"1956 Emmy Award Nominees and Winners." Emmys, www.emmys.com/awards/nominees-winners/1956.

"Antioch College. Carol Serling '50." Antioch College, Jan. 2020, antioch-college.edu/2020/01/carol-serling-50.

Associated Press. "On Bummy Davis." The New York Times, 18 Nov. 1979.

Berserk: The Shocking Life and Death of Edwin Valero. By Don Stradley. Hamilcar Noir, 2019.

Bloody Elbow. Nash, John S. "James Figg: The Lost Origins of the Sport of Mixed Martial Arts." 1 Nov. 2010.

Bonanza. Sugar, Bert Randolph. The 100 Greatest Boxers of All Time, 1984.

Boxing Scene Forum. boxingscene.com/forums/showthread.php?t=458393.

Boy Scout Wrestling Database. Cage Match Internet Wrestling Database, www.cagematch.net.

Brown Glove Books. Johnson, Catherine. Then The World Moved On: The Brutal Truth Behind the Max Baer–Frankie Campbell Fight, 2024.

Casey, Mike. "From New Orleans To New York: Unforgettable Tony Canzoneri." Cyber Boxing Zone, www.cyberboxingzone.com.

Casey, Mike. "Jack Sharkey." Cyber Boxing Zone, 8 Apr. 2009.

Champion. Written by Carl Foreman, directed by Mark Robson, United Artists, 1949.

Champion. Written by Rod Serling, directed by Allen Reisner, Climax!, 31 Mar. 1955. The Paley Center for Media, www.paleycenter.org/collection/item/?q=rod+serling&item=T:16193.

Chuck. Written by Michael Cristofer, Jeff Feuerzeig, Liev Schreiber, and Jerry Stahl. Directed by Phillippe Falardeau. IFC Films, 2016.

"Chuck Connors, Did You Know." OurChuckConnors.com, www.ourchuckconnors.com/did-you-know.html.

Dempsey, Jack. "I Can Whip Any Mechanical Robot." Modern Mechanix, Apr. 1934.

Ecco. McRae, Donald. Heroes Without a Country: America's Betrayal of Joe Louis and Jesse Owens, 2002.

Esquire. Lardner, Ring. "Champion." July 1949.

Fitzgerald, Mike. The Ageless Warrior: The Life of Boxing Legend Archie Moore. Sports Publishing LLC, 2004.

Friedman, Ian C. Latino Athletes. Facts on File, 2007.

Gates, Gary P. "Requiem For a Heavyweight Gives Quinn Another Challenging Role." Hamilton Speculator, 12 Mar. 1962.

George, Clarence. "Jack Palance: A Backseat to Baksi." Boxing.com, 6 Aug. 2014.

Grams, Martin Jr. The Twilight Zone: Unlocking the Door to a Television Classic. OTR Publishing, 2008.

Grams, Martin Jr. "The Radio Career of Rod Serling." OTRR.org, www.otrr.org/.../The_Radio_Career_Of_Rod_Serling.html.

Heller, Peter. In This Corner: Forty World Champions Tell Their Stories. Simon & Schuster, 1973.

Hoch, Edward D. "The Ring With the Velvet Ropes." In Rod Serling's Night Gallery Reader, Dembner Books, 1987.

Hypertextbook. "The Physics Factbook: Number of Televisions in the US", hypertextbook.com/facts/2007/TamaraTamazashvili.shtml.

Jewish Heroes and Heroines in America. Brody, Seymour "Sy." "Max. M. Novich: The Dean Of Sports Medicine." seymourbrody.com/heroes_wwii/br113.htm.

"Joy True. Olde Epping: NH's Heavyweight Boxing Champ of the World." Seacoast Online, 4 July 2019.

Little, Brown. Serling, Rod. "Eyes." The Season To Be Wary, 1967.

Losers: The Miscast Champion. Written by Brin-Jonathan Butler. Directed by Mickey Duzyj. Netflix, 1 Mar. 2019.

Louis, Joe. My Life. Harcourt, 1978.

MarinFireHistory.com. Lellis, William. "Boxing, Murder, and Firefighting, Oh My!" www.marinfirehistory.org.

Million Dollar Baby. Written by Paul Haggis. Directed by Clint Eastwood. Warner Bros. Pictures, 2004.

Modern Mechanix. "Robots Stage Realistic Prize Fight." Apr. 1933.

Mulvaney, Kieran. "Submitted For Your Approval: Mike Tyson and The Twilight Zone." Boxing Scene, 18 Nov. 2024.

New England Historical Society. "We Wuz Robbed, or How Jack Sharkey Boxed His Way to a Catchphrase." 2017.

One Man Tango. Quinn, Anthony. Harper Collins, 1995.

Our Chuck Connors. www.ourchuckconnors.com.

Parisi, Nicholas. Rod Serling: His Life, Work, and Imagination. University Press of Mississippi, 2018.

"Papke Career Ends With Murder, Suicide." San Pedro News Pilot, 27 Nov. 1936.

"Professional Boxing Hearings Before the Subcommittee..." U.S. Senate, 1960.

Query, Vanessa. "Rod Serling at Antioch College." Yellow Springs News, 4 Aug. 2010, ysnews.com.

Raging Bull. Written by Paul Schrader and Mardik Martin. Directed by Martin Scorsese. United Artists, 1980.

The Set-Up. Written by Art Cohn. Directed by Robert Wise. RKO, 1949.

Serling, Anne. As I Knew Him: My Dad, Rod Serling. Citadel, 2013.

Serling, Rod. Patterns. Simon and Schuster, 1957.

Serling, Rod. Requiem for a Heavyweight. Bantam Books, 1962.

Serling, Rod. "The Big, Tall Wish." More Stories from The Twilight Zone, Bantam, 1961.

Simon, John. "Theater/Little Week of Horrors." New York Magazine, 18 Mar. 1985.

Skelton, Scott, and Jim Benson. Rod Serling's Night Gallery: An After-Hours Tour. Syracuse University Press, 1998.

Stallone, Sylvester. Rocky. Dir. John Avildsen. United Artists, 1976.

Stallone, Sylvester. Rocky II. United Artists, 1979.

Steel. Written by Richard Matheson. The Twilight Zone, 4 Oct. 1963.

Stradley, Don. Berserk: The Shocking Life and Death of Edwin Valero. Hamilcar Noir, 2019.

Szkotak, Steve. "Ex-Champ Jack Sharkey Nears 81st Birthday." UPI Archives, 8 Oct. 1983.

Tell It to Groucho. YouTube, uploaded 16 Feb. 2016, www.youtube.com/watch?v=7AuR8WLd_ac&t=173s.

The Twilight Rounds. Written by Rod Serling. Dir. Maury Holland. Kraft Theatre, 27 May 1953. The Paley Center for Media.

The Twilight Zone: A Short Drink From a Certain Fountain. Written by Rod Serling. Dir. Bernard Girard. 13 Dec. 1963.

The Twilight Zone: The Big, Tall Wish. Written by Rod Serling. Dir. Ron Winston. 8 Apr. 1960.

The Twilight Zone: The Four of Us Are Dying. Written by Rod Serling. Dir. John Brahm. 1 Jan. 1960.

The Twilight Zone: The Sixteen-Millimeter Shrine. Written by Rod Serling. Dir. Mitchell Leisen. 23 Oct. 1959.

Weaver, Tom. "Woman of the Apes." Starlog Magazine, no. 213, Apr. 1995.

CHRISTOPHER BENEDICT

Weinstein, Matt. "Sharkey Became World Heavyweight Champion 82 Years Ago Saturday." PressConnects, 21 June 2014.

Wrestling Scout. sites.google.com/site/wrestlingscout.

Zicree, Marc Scott. The Twilight Zone Companion: Second Edition. Silman-James Press, 1992.

About the Author

Christopher Benedict (pictured above with Anne Serling) lives in Huntington, New York—birthplace of Walt Whitman and former hometown of Gerry Cooney—a writer and a fighter, fittingly enough.

In addition to *The Twilight Rounds*, Benedict has self-published six books on boxing over the last decade: *Mandatory Eight Count, Resuming Hostilities, Hooking Off The Jab, Punching Through Boxing's Glass Ceiling, You Can't Smash Stereotypes By Staying in the Neutral Corner*, and *I'm Not In The Business. I Am The Business.*

A longtime advocate for women's boxing, Chris' writings on the subject are now being featured and preserved on the WBAN (Women's Boxing Archive Network) Historical Database, founded and maintained by trailblazing female prizefighter Sue 'Tiger Lilly' Fox.

An elector for both the International Boxing Hall of Fame and International Women's Boxing Hall of Fame, Benedict is also a member of *The Ring* magazine's women's boxing ratings panel and served as a contributing archive researcher for the 2023 documentary *Right To Fight*.

In September 2024, he was a featured presenter at *SerlingFest: A Serling Centennial*, where he delivered a lecture based on this book at the Forum Theatre in Rod Serling's hometown of Binghamton. A lifelong enthusiast of monster movies and science fiction, Chris also wrote a book of essays on these beloved genres called *Needs Must When the Devil Drives*, which begins with a lengthy look inside Rod Serling's involvement in 1968's *Planet of the Apes*.

As always, thanks for reading!

Chris' six previous titles are self-published compilations of his boxing writings spanning the years 2015-2023.

For more details, or to obtain a copy of any of these books, please contact the author at cwbene@gmail.com.

Also From Jobber House Press:

The Twilight Zone Haiku:
Poems Inspired by the Landmark Television Series

Kaiju Haiku:
A Haiku Comics Zine, Illustrated by Jason McBride

Muay Thai Kickboxing:
The Ultimate Guide to Conditioning Training and Fighting

Kaiju and Kayfabe:
Japanese Giant Monster Cinema and Professional Wrestling

www.ingramcontent.com/pod-product-compliance
Lightning Source LLC
Chambersburg PA
CBHW070334130626
46556CB00007B/2856